Meeting Emma

Meeting Emma

A story of spiritual discovery

Michael Spyker

Authentic

Copyright 2004 Michael Spyker

10 09 08 07 06 05 04   7 6 5 4 3 2 1

First published in 2004 by Authentic Media,
9 Holdom Avenue, Bletchley, Milton Keynes, MK1 1QR, UK
and
P.O. Box 1047, Waynesboro, GA 30830-2047, USA
www.authenticmedia.co.uk

British Library Cataloguing in Publication Data
A catalogue record for this book is available from the
British Library

ISBN 1-85078-587-2

Cover Design by Peter Barnsley
Typeset by WestKey Ltd, Falmouth, Cornwall
Print Management by Adare Carwin
Printed and bound by AIT Nørhaven A/S, Denmark

TO SASKIA
who is as much like Emma,
as anyone else might be.

Read with hurry,
as you worry,
'bout your many daily chores.
Read with pleasure,
at your leisure,
and discover distant shores.

Contents

Preface

Every person has a spiritual story to tell, and when a discussion takes place about spirituality it will involve human experience. Stories will differ, of course, and much will depend on culture, background and fate. For Christians their story will be greatly influenced by what they believe about God and how they have come to know God. It is also influenced by how much is known about the great spiritual traditions and practices of the church over the past 2,000 years. This wealth of wisdom and opportunity in reaching out to God has remained for many somewhat hidden and only recently, due in part to a heightened interest in spirituality in society at large, is it beginning to emerge.

There is much to be gained by being familiar with the options available for relating with God. People haven't changed much over the years and God is the same yesterday, today and for ever. What was helpful years ago with regard to prayer and spiritual exercises is still helpful today. Much can be learned from those who have walked by faith before us. The information in this book is not new. But it may have its surprises.

Spirituality is story. A list of spiritual principles and ideas that are interesting may be helpful, but will lack the factor of human engagement. It is with this in mind that *Meeting Emma* has been written as a story around two main characters: Emma and Joe. It is their story, but not theirs alone, for ideas and experiences are discussed with which many a Christian will identify.

The book is meant to read very easily. But at the same time the reader may find it necessary to go over the ground again, because there is so much contained in the text. It is the kind of book, I hope, that one can revisit regularly. Readers may find that it assists them in keeping the search for a vibrant spiritual life well on track.

Finally, *Meeting Emma* has not been written solely for people who go to church. Those who no longer do so may find much in it that is valuable. Emma herself has dropped out of church and Joe helps her to rekindle an active relationship with Jesus Christ. *Meeting Emma* is not a 'religious' book. Those simply interested in what Christianity has on offer spiritually will find it informative. It is a story about life and health and spiritual reality. A story that should make for a good read. I hope that you will enjoy it.

Michael Spyker, Adelaide, 2004

PS In the Appendix entitled 'Walking the Walk' (p. 125), you will find additional information relating to each chapter with some questions for personal reflection and/or group discussion.

1

Coffee

Meeting Joseph Christobello would change Emma's life. But of course she didn't know that.

'You paint,' he said, appearing at the small pavement table in a busy shopping arcade where Emma regularly drank coffee and made drawings.

'No, I draw, actually.' She kept her gaze on her drawing pad. Such interruptions were a minor nuisance. Fortunately they didn't happen often.

'But where does it come from, that drawing?'

There was a moment of hesitant silence, uncertain of further engagement.

'From my hand.'

'Ah.'

Her concentration was gone. 'Do I know you?' she asked, looking up at a middle-aged man with a twinkle in his eye.

'You might. We met six months ago. At Tanya Lawson's twenty-first. You're Emma, aren't you? I'm Joe.'

Now she remembered. Joe was a family friend of the Lawsons. Tanya had spoken of him appreciatively. Emma and Joe had had a brief discussion that evening at the party.

'Hello, Joe. Nice to see you again.' She was intrigued by his question. As an artist she knew, of course, that her hand's creativity originated inside her. But she had never given it overly much thought.

Joe was looking at the drawing on the table. He seemed hesitant, as if ready to walk on but not quite willing to do so, as if walking on would be somehow inappropriate.

'Why did you ask that question about my drawing?' Later, Emma could not decide what made her continue the conversation. Perhaps it was fate – or just plain curiosity.

'Perhaps I shouldn't have,' Joe replied after a few seconds. Making smart comments whatever the situation would get him into real trouble one day, he reflected. He was suddenly in two minds. He would have cut this meeting short, but Emma was looking at him expectantly and it would be unkind to walk on.

'But you did ask it.'

He smiled. 'Yes. It's the important question of being before doing.'

'Oh.' She looked at him enquiringly.

'Can I get you another coffee, perhaps?'

For a moment Emma wondered if she was being chatted up by an older man. But that wasn't what was happening, she decided. Joe seemed a nice enough person. They'd already met, they had mutual friends and they'd chatted together before.

'That would be nice.'

Joe made his way to the coffee bar, and Emma resumed her artist's eye scrutiny of the street.

The sun stood brightly in the stark blue sky and fell upon everything with a vividness of colour of which she would never tire. It hit Emma deeply with unspeakable effects and fed a submerged frustration. It was so far beyond, so much deeper than anything she could ever creatively put on paper. Real art is larger than life, Emma had once concluded. But even so, to really live would somehow definitely be larger than art.

A fresh cappuccino was placed in front of her.

'I love summer.' Joe sat down and stirred his coffee. 'You sure you don't mind?' he asked. Emma shook her head.

'As an artist you must have wondered about the deeper things of life.' Joe had no intention of beating about the bush with this conversation. It would either be meaningful, or it wouldn't happen at all. He never was any good at small talk anyway.

'I'm just an art *student*, for now.' In Emma's own mind she was indeed an artist. But at the age of twenty-two, it was sometimes safer to call yourself a student.

'I see.' Joe sat back and relaxed. He was beginning to like Emma's frankness. The age difference between them was such that she could easily have been his daughter; but he liked young people and made no apologies for liking them. His first remarks to her had been spontaneous and unpremeditated. Now, he decided, he was going to take the encounter seriously and continue the interaction unless she cut it short.

'Yes, I have wondered about life,' Emma said.

'I'm sure you have. For an artist it's essential. For everyone, actually.'

Emma looked out into the street and decided to change the conversation.

'The colours, in the sunlight. They hit me every time.'

'Yes. That's because you're someone who senses what it should be like to really "be". Real being is the essence of personhood. Unfortunately not many ever discover their full potential.'

Joe seemed bent on pursuing the life-and-being issue, rather than the brightness of the colours around them. Emma ignored his explanation.

'I can feel those colours.'

'You're fortunate, Emma.'

Emma fell silent. Joe too momentarily lost the desire to talk. He enjoyed colour as well. He always did.

Something was troubling Emma. The conversation was becoming rather philosophical, and she'd had some bad experiences with philosophy lately: people trying to mess with her mind. New Agers – there were a few of those on campus. It was one part of student life she had become weary of.

'Where do your ideas about reality come from?'

Joe was struck by her perceptiveness. 'That's a fair question. From years of study, and the wisdom of Christianity,' he explained.

'You're a Christian?'

'Yes, I confess that I am. Do you know much about Christianity?'

'Quite a bit. Sure. I used to go to church. I don't go any more, but I'm not anti-Christian.'

Church had never done her much harm. She had been a churchgoer for years: she'd even attended a few Christian holiday camps. It had all been fun and meaningful, especially because her two best friends had been there too. But they had moved on now. One had moved away from the area, and the other had married. Everything had changed. In due course Emma herself had left town to go to university in the city.

The church had actually done quite a good job. She knew the youth leaders best. She barely knew the minister at all, apart from occasional quick hellos and when she got baptised. When her circle of friends broke up sooner than expected, she had been at a loose end. She got over it.

The church service was OK, she decided, but it sent out a message that over the years had become largely predictable. Sure, there had been moments during those years in which she actually experienced what she would call 'faith'. Church had been helpful for that reason. But it hadn't happened very often, certainly not enough to keep her at meetings every week.

At university Emma had made new friends. Not quite as close as the first group, but decent enough. She occasionally thought back on church with nostalgia and moments of regret that things had to change so much. She was convinced it would be harder to get satisfaction out of church these days than when she was younger and more impressionable.

She had belief, somewhere; it had never fully left her. But it was easy to ignore it. Jesus had meaning, for sure. Still; whatever it was, however it worked, her faith – as she still called it – lived on a slow burner, rather hidden, and seeming to be almost second-hand.

Joe broke into her reverie. 'We were talking about colours. Do you see that pale yellow wall there, with the terracotta window?'

Emma followed his gaze to a wall across the street. She knew it quite well. Some months earlier she had drawn it, with a few people walking past it. Perhaps one day she'd try again. The wall projected a presence. It was one of the better sights in the street.

'That wall has a kind of perfect form for me,' Joe explained. He loved talking about architecture.

'You feel quite strongly about it,' Emma remarked.

'Yes. It reminds me of the Shakers.'

'The Shakers?'

'A religious group. They lived in the USA quite some years ago. They built beautiful buildings and made furniture with a combination of perfect form and simplicity. Your library should have some books about them.'

He paused, still looking towards the yellow wall and the patterns of shade that the sun made on it. 'I don't know why it is so beautiful. It just is.' He took a sip of coffee. His cup was empty.

'You are looking at art,' she suggested. Emma was serious about her art, and she knew a little about human perception.

'You're right.' Joe had studied neither art nor architecture, but appreciated them both.

'Are you a teacher, Joe?' It seemed a reasonable guess.

'Yes – of sorts. Only not at a school.'

'What do you teach?'

'Spirituality. Christian Spirituality, to be precise.'

'Oh.' Emma digested the information. 'Why does that subject interest you?'

Joe considered a variety of answers before deciding on: 'Because it deals with people, and with being really yourself.'

'The deeper things of life. That's what you called them before.'

Joe smiled. 'Yes, that's it.'

'Is it religious?' Emma asked.

Joe recognised instantly what she meant. He was familiar with the distinction young people often made between being 'spiritual' but not 'religious'.

'No, I don't think so. A bit the opposite, actually, I would think.'

'You teach at a church?'

'No, a college.'

Emma picked up one of her pencils. It was a spontaneous reaction. Joe looked at his watch.

'I'd love to tell you more Emma, but I need to move on. Thanks for letting me have a coffee with you.' He stood up. 'Do you often sit here drawing?'

'For the next two weeks, most days.'

'So I might bump into you again?'

'Sure,' said Emma without hesitation. 'If you like.'

'I would.'

With that Joe was on his way. Emma's eyes followed him for a while down the busy street as he weaved through a crowd of shoppers.

2

Who Is It, That I Am?

A week later, the sun still shining in a sky faintly scattered with clouds, Joe was walking down the street towards his favourite bookstore. He told himself that he was doing so to see whether anything new and interesting had hit the shelves. But that was Plan B. His main purpose was to see if Emma was drawing at the coffee shop. After all, he had sort of promised that he would pass by; and he had quite enjoyed their previous conversation. She might have changed her mind about meeting again. That would be fine too. But there was only one way to find out.

Emma was sitting at the same table as before. But she did not notice him approaching. Her concentration was focused on her drawing; she had eyes only for that. Joe, who always found it fascinating to watch artists at work, debated for a moment about walking on. But he decided to stay, and as he made the decision, Emma's concentration loosened up a little.

'Hello, Emma.'

She looked up, smiled. 'Hi Joe.' She seemed happy to take a break. 'Have a seat.'

'Would you like a drink?' Joe asked. 'I'm getting a coffee.'

'Just water, thanks.'

Emma had been wondering whether Joe would make the effort to meet again. Probably he would, she guessed, but she couldn't be sure. Life wasn't quite that predictable. She had enjoyed their previous conversation. It had been different and in a way stimulating. And it had brought back memories. Lately, her feelings had been prompting her to an unaccustomed spiritual reflection: she had become aware of troubling unresolved questions in her mind, things she hadn't thought about since her church-going days. She had even started reading her Bible again, but it didn't grab her much. And for some reason, that had irritated her, though she didn't know why.

Joe reappeared with his coffee and a glass of water and sat down. 'How's it going?' He nodded towards the drawing.

'Struggling,' Emma confessed. 'I have to submit a drawing with the title "Existence". It's difficult.'

'I see,' said Joe. 'That allows for all sorts.'

'Yes, but to chose a subject and then bring a particular kind of life to it, that's what's hard.' Emma suddenly looked tired. It had been a demanding week.

'Existence,' Joe reflected. 'To be, or not to be.' He sipped his coffee carefully. It was hot.

'Yes. Or – ' There was a small pause. 'I am who I am.' Emma's response surprised herself. Somehow it had just popped out. She watched for Joe's reaction, expecting him to recognise the quote. He looked at her sideways, his cup still near his lips.

'Yes, that's the more significant one,' he conceded. 'But – who is it, that I am?'

'You like playing with words, don't you?'

'Sometimes. Words can be rather important.'

Emma let the comment pass unanswered. Instead she broached a subject that she had been thinking about since their last meeting. 'You mentioned last time about being – about "being" before "doing".'

'Ah,' said Joe, for he did remember.

'So you must have specific ideas about it?'

'Yes, I do,' Joe admitted.

Emma made no further comment.

'OK, for what it's worth, then,' he continued. 'Being really ourselves is important. Much of what we do and how we act derives from it. But who are we? Who, actually, am I? Who I think that I am, shapes my identity. My personal confidence is based on it.'

Joe looked at Emma. She seemed interested, so he continued. 'If I feel OK about myself, I will be more able to be my own person. If however I am unsure about myself, then how I go about my business will to a large extent be determined by the influences and demands of others, rather than by my own ideas of who I really feel I'd like to be. Thomas Merton calls this our "social compulsions". Of course, it's quite possible for me to think that I'm sort of OK, while in certain areas I'm actually not. And that complicates matters further.'

'Come again?' Emma said.

'Yes, sure,' Joe continued. 'Sorry, that was a little much in a few sentences. Well – from childhood we all grow up with messages that people and culture put into our heads. Like, for instance, that being number one is important; and that being significant is greatly helped by looking attractive. Heaps of messages. And of course, as a result, we begin to have our own messages, our self-talk, much of which can be quite damaging as it may be negative, defensive, or arrogant.'

Joe reached for his coffee.

'We all have those messages?' Emma asked, though she knew the answer quite well from experience.

'Yes, we do. The simple fact is that we all try to cope by dealing with the messages as best we can. If we feel we're doing OK, we can usually find ourselves some inner peace. But if deep down we feel that we are not coping well, then our thoughts and emotions will often oppress and suppress us, instead of encouraging us. We'll be more vulnerable to the negative stuff that goes on in our heads, than we need to be.'

'You mean that I am myself, but not really myself, as a result of all those messages?' Emma was trying to come to grips with the idea and her response was perceptive.

'Well, yes – and no.'

'Go on.'

'Yes, because of course these messages exist. No, because there is much more to people than the messages they accumulate over the years. The message bank is still powerful though. More so than you might think.'

'Who is Thomas Merton?' Emma felt the need to change the conversation a little. She had heard Merton's name before; but where, she could not remember. Perhaps a university friend had mentioned him.

'A famous Catholic monk.'

'Famous for what?'

'For his writings. Many people, not just Christians, have benefited from them. He died in the sixties – he was accidentally electrocuted in his hotel. A faulty electric fan.' Joe wondered whether the comment about Merton's unfortunate premature death was entirely relevant. It sounded like gossip, he told himself, and he silently rebuked himself.

Emma stood up. 'I think I'll get a juice. You want another coffee?'

'I'm OK, thanks.'

A girl called Nicky, whom Emma knew socially, was serving behind the counter. Curiosity about Emma's older companion was clearly written on Nicky's face, but Emma didn't explain. She felt no particular need to, and her thoughts were elsewhere. She recognised that Joe was taking the discussion in a certain direction. But how far should she follow along, and what was the best attitude to adopt? It could get quite personal with all that talk about 'being' and 'identity'. Should she open herself up to that?

As she made her way back to her table, Emma made a decision. She would lower her defences a little. Joe seemed a reasonable person, and anyway, she could always pull back if necessary. She resumed her seat and before putting her juice down, she closed her drawing pad. After all, there was no point risking a spill and ruining her work.

Joe had made a decision too.

'I could tell you lots of things, Emma. In fact, I like talking about these matters – they're important. At least I think they are; knowing what I know has made a world of difference in my own life.' He paused and looked frankly at Emma. 'But to really benefit from understanding these matters, you need to do more than just talk. There are ways to increase your inner peace and awareness of self that really work. Of course you can go into bookshops and find shelves full of books that offer suggestions, but that's not what I'm talking about. The way forward that really works for me is with God.'

He paused. Emma made no comment. She was looking thoughtfully at her orange juice.

'The thing is,' Joe continued, 'that whatever I talk to you about – which could be a great deal – isn't of much real use unless you are prepared to engage your faith and try some reflective spiritual exercises.' He wondered whether he had gone too far; he might have lost Emma's willingness to stay with the topic. Then he would have to change the subject.

But Emma was intent on following the flow of the discussion, even though it was taking an unexpected turn. 'That will minimise the messages we talked about?'

'Yes – and much more.'

'OK.'

'You may have to spend real quality time with yourself,' Joe explained.

'You mean being more on my own?'

'You can be on your own a lot, without ever really being with yourself,' said Joe. 'Many people don't actually like being with themselves, and try to avoid it.'

That was not Emma's problem. True, sometimes she could get annoyed with herself when alone and unoccupied. But she regularly needed personal space to mull things over. She'd found that the best way to achieve that was to find a quiet place somewhere, or a place where nobody knew her.

'I don't mind being on my own, thinking about things,' she said. 'I often put some music on and just relax.' Unless, as often happened, the peace was disturbed by her housemates crashing in. Quiet could come at a premium.

'Excellent,' Joe responded. 'But who do you relax *with*?'

'What do you mean? Nobody. Just myself.'

'Yes, of course.' Joe was contrite. 'Sorry, Emma. I was trying to be clever. Look, I was speaking as a Christian. I'm never really, completely, by myself. That's what's special about Christianity, you see. Christians are in a relationship with Jesus Christ. We may not think much about it, but he is totally involved with us.'

'So how about when you're doing your own thing – maybe even something bad?'

'Makes no difference. The Spirit of Christ lives in you. You don't have two spirits, in some sort of split existence –

one for when you do things with Jesus, another for when you're not; he is always engaged.'

'Sure,' Emma agreed cautiously. This was an idea that needed further thought.

'So when you are relaxing and thinking about things, having all your self-talk, you may as well recognise that Jesus is part of the process and talk with him as well. Not necessarily *always* talking – he knows your thoughts anyway. The aim is just to be relational with him. Think of him and be intuitive in your feelings.'

'And what does that achieve?'

'He helps. Don't ask me exactly how, for that I can't say.'

'He helps …' Emma repeated, more to herself than to Joe.

I could accept that, she thought. When she was a member of the Youth Group she'd experienced Jesus' help more than once. She had always felt that Jesus was never far away; and even now, that feeling was still there, though now deeply submerged.

'If you want to become more like your real self, Emma,' said Joe, 'he is the one who can make it happen. Nobody else can, whatever they might say. That's what's so great about the Christian life. But there are stages you need to go through and things you need to do, if you are to arrive at a complete discovery of self.'

Time was moving on.

'Emma, you told me that you listen to music while you're relaxing.'

She nodded absently, still thinking about those times when Jesus seemed to have been closer.

'I was wondering – would you consider trying a simple spiritual exercise?'

'What do you mean?'

'Well – one good way of settling down with yourself is by using music that relaxes you. You can just play it as background, or you can choose music that reminds you of something or someone.'

Music was important to Emma. When she was on her own she often had music playing, usually just music she liked, of no particular significance. Still, she was willing to try Joe's suggestions.

'Go on – what am I supposed to do?'

'Do you know the song "Come Away with Me", by Norah Jones? Can you get hold of a copy?'

'Yes, I can.' She knew the CD and liked it. It was clever and relaxing music.

'Next time you have a quiet time by yourself, play that CD. Listen particularly to that song,' explained Joe. 'And if you feel like it, allow Jesus into your space. Don't expect that anything special will necessarily happen, just give yourself the option of being with him.'

Joe looked out across the street, allowing Emma some space to think about his suggestion. After a moment she replied.

'Why would I do that?'

'Because you felt like it. Otherwise, please don't do it. If you decide against it – and that's fair enough – it's not a problem.' It was important, Joe knew, that the idea should be freely taken up. Otherwise there would be little point and it might even be counterproductive.

'OK.' Emma left her response hanging, without making it clear whether she was agreeing to the music or indeed to the spiritual exercise.

'And Emma, could we meet one more time – in a fort-night, perhaps? You don't have to, of course.'

She smiled. 'I could disappoint you with that music idea,' she said.

'No problem,' Joe replied. 'Whatever you decide, it's not personal.' From the way he spoke, Emma knew he meant it.

   'Can you let me have a piece of paper and a pencil?' Joe asked.

   Emma opened her drawing pad at a page of trial sketches she was going to throw away, and passed Joe a pencil. He scribbled something in the bottom corner. 'Some lines by St John of the Cross, who is known for his intimacy with Jesus. A bit like the Song of Solomon.' Joe explained.

   'Who is he?'

   'Another famous monk. From Spain this time. He died hundreds of years ago.'

   Emma laughed. 'Two monks in one day.'

   Joe got up, ready to move on. 'Same time, same place?'

   'Sure,' said Emma.

   'I like your drawings,' said Joe. 'Keep at it.'

   As Joe disappeared from her view, Emma began to decipher the three scribbled lines.

> How gently and lovingly
> you wake my heart
> where in secret you dwell alone.[1]
> *John of the Cross*

---

[1] 'The Living Flame of Love', in: K. Kavanaugh and O. Rodriguez (trs), *The Collected Works of St John of the Cross* (Institute of Carmelite Studies, 1994), 53

3

The Invitation

Emma had a headache. She felt lousy. Also, she had an hour to get ready for her part-time job and couldn't be bothered. But of course she would go because of the money. She knew that going out last night with friends and coming home in the early hours was partly to blame for how she felt, even though she didn't have a hangover. Emma hoped that the double-strength coffee she was sipping at the kitchen table might at least clear her head. Perhaps this was the beginning of a virus.

She hated it when she was in one of her less positive moods. I'll snap out of it later, she told herself, but not yet. No point denying your feelings. That was her mother talking; all very well, but feelings had never got her very far. If she had lived solely by feelings she might still be at home and sulking, instead of being at university and living in a major city.

Her life hadn't been all that difficult, but there was still plenty to deal with. Her father was often at sea in the navy. When he was home he treated his home and family like a ship and its crew. When Dad was away, Emma suspected, her mother had some fun of her own. Dad probably knew about it but wasn't a stranger himself to a bit on the side.

To their credit, they had stayed together for the children; and strangely enough, they were rather infatuated

with each other when they were together. But it had ran-
kled with Emma. Of course, she told herself, it was none of
her business. Except coping with the reality of it.

It was her art, really, that kept her on track. The struggle
it presented was one worth having. She looked forward
to the day she'd leave for Europe to visit the major art
centres. Her aunt, who was a landscape painter of some
note, had promised her a plane ticket and spending
money as a graduation gift. She'd learned of that amazing
offer on her twenty-first birthday. Before Europe was a lot
of work to be done. It was work she would surely manage.
Graduation was almost a certainty.

But even thinking about Europe didn't cheer her up
this morning. She was having the blues plus a headache
plus something else. Niggling questions had been troubling her for some time now: about life in general, about art,
and why bother? Or rather, how to best bother with it?
Such thoughts were not new to Emma but lately they
seemed to follow her around. It was a nuisance, and quite
stupid in a way. Student life hadn't given her much to
complain about, not if you compared it with what some of
her friends were facing. But unfortunately, that didn't
make much difference right now to how she felt.

She decided she'd better make some toast. She had a busy
day to look forward to and she needed something in her
stomach. Her problem, she realised, was an existential
one, about life and meaning. That's probably what growing up does to you, she told herself. If art was going to be
what she lived for, then that was more than fine by her. But
it wasn't quite enough. Art could be a slippery taskmaster.
Intuitively she felt that unless she was careful she could
end up becoming its slave rather than its dedicated practi-
tioner. If she was to stay with her craft as a person in a
healthy way, it must be as Emma involved with art: not as

Emma involved, yet in sufferance to the unattainable – the beauty of a perfect painting.

Where did such thoughts come from? She didn't know. But they were true enough, and she needed to find answers, she recognised. Emma could be philosophical about how she dealt with issues. But she was beginning to realise that solving this puzzle would not be easy. It would be a long-term struggle, similar to those 'messages' Joe had spoken of, but different.

And she was becoming increasingly frustrated with where she was living. It had seemed great when she moved in; places always did. Her housemates were fine, no problem there. Her room wasn't bad, either. But she felt as if she didn't belong in the house any more. That was stupid, for she'd only ever seen it as a convenient solution to an accommodation problem.

Her frustration lay much deeper. She had never felt entirely settled in any place, even in her family home, since she had found out about her mum and dad's 'arrangement'. When she had discovered it, while a teenager, something deep inside her had been badly shaken. A period of pain and mood swings followed. She'd never talked about it to her parents. What use would that have been?

But that was years ago: she should be over it now. I'm full of existential angst, Emma decided, with wry humour. She bit into a piece of toast. Really, she should snap out of this mood.

And now there was Joe. Another problem that possibly could be part of a solution. But was it a solution she'd want? To be honest, meeting Joe had been one of the better surprises. A month ago he had been an almost forgotten name, somebody met briefly at a party. Now he was teaching her 'spiritual exercises'.

He seemed to have a way of sensing what was going on in her mind. That was a little uncanny, but Emma suspected it was simply because he knew the things young people tend to struggle with and had some ideas about dealing with them. To his credit, he had openly declared his allegiance to Christianity right from the start.

And that at a time when she herself had begun hesitantly to reconsider her faith. Was it a coincidence? Or was Joe some kind of angel, a messenger from God? Emma had to smile. Some angel, she thought. All the same, the matter presented her with a further problem, and a more urgent one than the others. Should she reactivate her Christian belief? It was a serious question, for Emma did not believe in half measures.

Joe's suggestion of listening to music hadn't really worked. She had crashed down on her bed at the end of a pig of a day, put on a mellow Norah Jones CD, and proceeded to fall asleep. Her mind was full of things, her nerves on edge. That obviously hadn't helped produce reflective insights. Anyway, it was always difficult to move from being active and animated into some sort of calm where you could turn off your senses and thoughts. She could manage it sometimes, just in suspended awareness, but not very often.

How you made sure that those moments would happen more regularly, Emma didn't know. The last time it happened, not so long ago, a mild presence both gentle and encouraging had entered her room. From that moment on, quite unexpectedly, she had felt that she needed to rekindle her faith, and had started reading her Bible again. But she didn't allow for the necessary quiet and concentration and became frustrated with it. She could now recognise her mistake. If she really meant business, then reading would have to feature more prominently in her day.

She went to her room to look for some headache tablets – no point in suffering unnecessarily. The song 'Come Away with Me' began to play through her mind. She had got at least that far with Norah Jones's CD before falling asleep. It was a great song – a love song of course, and also an invitation. The kind of situation you dream about, being taken by a lover to a secret place, but one which was unlikely to happen. Still, Emma understood why Joe had suggested it. The words he had scribbled on her art pad, which she had reflected on briefly yesterday while making some sketches, held an additional clue. Whoever this John of the Cross was, he seemed to understand being intimate with Jesus and expressed it rather beautifully. For that, of course, was the invitation – intimacy with the Lord. An invitation, she felt, that was now uncompromisingly staring her in the face. A half-hearted response would not be acceptable. It was either in or out. There was nothing in between. Emma could be quite pragmatic at times; but not in this case. Pragmatism was inappropriate now.

Emma was beginning to sense what her answer to the invitation must be. The smartest thing to do, she concluded, was to trust Joe. And not only listen to him, but actively participate in the discussions. She definitely wasn't short of questions to ask. Joe, she expected, would suggest more 'spiritual exercises'. Well – in for a penny, in for a pound. Unless it all became ridiculous, she would give it a go, on condition that she could call a halt to the whole thing at any time. Joe wouldn't have any difficulty with that, Emma knew.

With two headache tablets safely swallowed and the Joe situation initially resolved, her headache was disappearing in more ways than one. Emma grabbed her bag for work and closed the front door behind her. It had begun to rain.

4

Meaning, Identity and Solitude

Joe really didn't know what to expect. He had come to the coffee shop early. He had a few minutes to spare, and he enjoyed using such time – rare, these days – to read books in such places. He had a book with him, and started to turn the pages as he wondered about Emma and what was ahead. He knew her well enough by now to be sure that she would turn up. But he had no idea of what sort of meeting it was going to be. He wouldn't blame her if she decided that the acquaintance had gone far enough. It would be unfortunate, but understandable. Joe reflected that he had been rather forthcoming with his advice; maybe overly so.

'Is it an interesting book?'

Emma sounded slightly hoarse. She was feeling rather off-colour.

'It's a detective story,' Joe smiled. 'Quite a good one. Let me get the drinks. Coffee?'

'No, let me,' protested Emma, but gracefully gave way when Joe insisted. She sat down.

'You haven't brought your sketch pad,' observed Joe, returning with two cups of coffee.

'Not today.' She had decided on her approach and was now deciding how up-front to be. Attack is often the best form of defence, though admittedly with Joe there wasn't much to be defensive about.

'Would you mind if I asked you a question?' Emma was stirring her coffee, directing her question more to the cup than to Joe.

'Sure.'

'Could you tell me about yourself?'

It was a reasonable request, and Joe was quietly pleased to hear it. It seemed that Emma had arrived with a plan. He leaned back into his chair and began. 'I'm married to Jane, and we have children. They've all left home now – one lives overseas. Both my wife and I became Christians some decades ago, and I eventually ended up as the minister of a small church. Right now I work for a theological college down the road.' He mentioned the name, and Emma nodded. She had heard of it.

'And how did your spirituality come about?' That was a key question for Emma. She hoped it would help her in finally deciding whether to continue meeting Joe.

'Slowly.' It was the word that came first to mind. Joe thought it was rather apt. Spiritual growth was a long process that could not be fast-forwarded, though there had been benefits from the start. 'When I became a Christian, my life changed. I'd found the piece of the puzzle that was missing. It was in my mid-twenties that I went through a period of seriously searching for foundational meaning. God answered that question and has done so ever since, more than adequately.' He sipped his coffee thoughtfully.

'The church I joined was lively and the worship was good. It was a charismatic fellowship and believed in healing prayer. To this day I don't have any argument with any of that, but over the years – and with the Holy Spirit's guidance – I have grown towards the quieter side of Christian experience. That church didn't offer me that. There's no reason why the charismatic and the contemplative can't function together, but you don't see it happen often. And it's nonsense to say, as some people do, that older people prefer the quieter experiences and that you should really be a younger person if you want to engage primarily with the livelier side of worship. I know plenty of young people who enjoy their reflective moments with God and find them most beneficial.'

'You mean meditation?' Emma had always been interested in meditation and had practised it a little.

'Exactly. But that's only one aspect of a much broader spectrum. There is lots more.'

'Anyway,' he continued, 'to complete the picture; I have learned and studied much. I appreciate better now the variety of spiritual expression and worship available in the Christian tradition. There are many insights and practices I never heard of before.'

Joe fell silent. Emma was deep in thought.

'And yes,' he resumed, 'perhaps most importantly of all, the journey has really helped me to find myself. I feel more integrated and at ease. I am far from perfect, of course – many people can vouch for that! But I'm not muddled up like so many other people, including some Christians. Still, I won't take credit for that. It's happened by the grace of God.'

'That was helpful. Thanks,' said Emma. 'Joe, I've been doing some thinking. I'd like to hear more of what you have to say. There are questions I want to ask. And I'll try some of the exercises, if you think that will be helpful. But if I decide to pull out, then I will.'

'That's fine by me,' said Joe.

'There's another thing. I used to think of myself as having faith. I want to have a faith again.'

Joe didn't comment on that. Instead he asked, 'Is there something in particular you'd like to talk about?'

'Yes. You told me that you were looking for meaning in life.'

'I was. That's a good point. It's essential to who we are as persons.' It was probably where Joe would have chosen to continue the discussion himself.

'I believe', Joe began, 'that significant meaning is given – you don't acquire it by thinking about it. It anchors itself into your spirit as a revelation, so that you know that you know that you know. And then that revelation influences your thoughts, your perceptions and your identity. Many people never experience such a revelation.'

'So how do they find meaning?' Emma asked.

'With difficulty. They often feel that something is missing. They construct meaning, through the ideas they hold about life, through their feelings and through their opinions. That's fine; but it's a shallow foundation to build a life on. People who are relational, who like to be involved with others, enjoy a good interactive family life or have a real feel for nature, have an advantage; meaning, in essence, is relational. A good interaction with people and creation can be very beneficial. But it still usually falls short of actual revelation.'

'So – finding real meaning in life comes by revelation,' Emma repeated.

'Yes. And revelation is always given. It comes from somewhere else, from outside of yourself.'

'And for a Christian, it is given by God.' Emma had worked that out quite easily. It seemed obvious.

'Yes; and once given it always remains. But of course you need to keep it alive.'

'So it can disappear?' Emma asked.

'Yes – if "disappear" means "become no longer visible". It doesn't mean it's gone. But the revelation can become submerged, and have less effect.'

'And then the meaning question will begin to bother you badly.' Emma had deduced that from her own experiences.

'Yes. You'll feel less grounded in your identity, because identity and meaning are interrelated.' Joe was trying hard to keep it simple without compromising accuracy.

'I should make some notes,' Emma said. 'Just a minute – I'll ask Nicky for some paper.' She went over to the counter, returning with a notepad and a pen. 'Can you go over the basic points again?' She jotted them down as he summarised them. 'I'll get an exercise book for these discussions.'

'So: meaning gets to the heart of who you are as a person. If life is to be meaningful it's essential to know what you are about. It also helps if you learn to live in peace with yourself.'

'That sounds impossible,' responded Emma, only partly tongue-in-cheek.

'It is,' Joe agreed. 'On your own, you haven't got a chance.'

'Oh.'

'But we're not on our own, are we?'

'No!' Emma remembered their previous conversation. 'Once a Christian – Jesus is always involved.'

'Exactly.' Joe nodded. 'But it's not easy to discover who we are essentially. I have my cultural background, my genetic code, my personality, my intelligence and so on. I will never, ever, be able to fully understand myself, for that's impossible. The best I can hope for can only be achieved with the help of God. Actually, my true identity is found in God.'

'So without God I can't really become myself?'

'Christianity teaches that you can't. Do you remember, I mentioned Thomas Merton last time? He was very strong on this point.'

Emma let the point sink in for a while, and scribbled down some of the information.

'There's another very important point,' said Joe.

'OK.'

'Self-understanding is arrived at privately. It may seem an obvious point, but many people never get to know themselves really well because they do not spend the time with themselves to find out. They're always busy doing something, or they have something keeping them busy. Others deliberately avoid looking at themselves because they are apprehensive about what they might see. Many people find their identity not from deep inside themselves – from who they *are* – but from what they *do*, and the jobs they have. There's a vast difference between the two.'

'Being before doing,' Emma commented.

'Yes, the "I am" is more fundamental than the "I do".'

'I need to take a break,' said Emma.

'Me too,' said Joe. 'Shall we stop for now?'

'No, not really. It's interesting. I'm going to buy you another coffee.'

When she got back from the counter, Joe asked if she had an e-mail address. 'I'd like to e-mail you something about prayer. It might be useful.' Emma scribbled down her e-mail address and the number of her mobile. He gave her his own details in return.

'I want to discuss the topic of solitude,' Joe said. 'But let me first add a last point about shaping identity as a Christian.'

Emma readied her pencil. Joe paced his speaking, allowing her time to make notes. 'OK, if the real me is in Jesus, and if I need to be discovered, it follows that I will find out who I really am by spending time with him privately and intimately. It would be good to write this next sentence down word for word, as you've got the notepad.'

Emma carefully wrote it down as directed. 'Unless I learn to become intimate with Jesus, my true self will never be sufficiently actualised.'

'Sorry – I'm beginning to sound like a lecturer,' Joe said apologetically. 'I appreciate how you stick with my line of thought, Emma. A lot of people would have opted out by now.'

Emma felt tired, and she hadn't felt too good to start with at the beginning of the conversation. But she could handle a little more. 'Go on, Joe. This is really helpful.'

'Just a last word about solitude. Solitude is the skill of being alone in a particular way. A modern theologian called Paul Tillich has said that language gives us the word "loneliness" to describe the pain of being alone – and the word "solitude" to describe the glory of being alone. That's well put.'

'Let me write that down,' Emma said. She rather liked it.

'Not many people purposely seek out solitude today. But in the fourth and fifth century, 1,600 years ago, many thousands of Christians began to live in the deserts of Egypt, Syria and Palestine in search of solitude. They considered society very corrupt and got away from it as far as possible. Their aim was to seek God in the quiet. They were given the collective name of Desert Fathers, or Desert Mothers. Today we still have ancient stories of their single-mindedness towards God and their wisdom. They knew how to practise solitude.'

'But I live in a city,' said Emma.

'Yes. Another writer, Henri Nouwen, encourages us to learn from the example of the desert,[1] even so.'

'How do I manage that?'

---

[1] H. Nouwen, *The Way of the Heart* (London: Daybreak, 1990)

'Not easily! Let me add an important point before we go on. Whatever we may talk about together regarding Christian spirituality are not things you just go out and do. It will take time, and you may never experience some things as others have. But I believe in being aware of what's on offer and giving it a go. You'll undoubtedly benefit from it. Some things may really work for you. But there are no easy answers.'

Emma nodded. Joe went on,

'Solitude starts with being alone, away from it all, and bringing yourself to rest. You try to stop thinking about issues and let yourself drift quietly, as it were, into the presence of Jesus. That's all, really. When it works out it's a quite glorious experience, which carries a meaning with it entirely its own. You just intuitively allow yourself to perceive what God may be telling you, if anything. God doesn't necessarily have to say something.

'Now here's what is interesting. If you do this regularly, you will find that you are beginning to carry a space with you: a kind of subtle distance that seems to exist between you, recollected in yourself, and wherever you are. Your environment doesn't dictate as it used to, though you are fully aware of it and what is going on. And you are continually aware of God's presence. You feel more your real self. In that way, you can be in solitude even in a busy shopping arcade.'

'And that works?' Emma asked.

'Yes, it does! But I have just described the ultimate. I can't live like that myself, but I do experience moments of it. And that's wonderful … But like I said, it's a long road.'

'So, what do I do?'

'I suggest you don't worry about it, but simply start with spending time quietly with Jesus. See what he has to say perhaps.'

'On the road of self-discovery.'

'Yes. If you like, we can talk about that further, but it will have to be in three weeks' time or later. I'll be out of town.'

Three weeks was fine by Emma.

5

The Prayer Spectrum

From: *Joe Christobello* [jchristobello@college.ac.uk]
To: *Emma*
Subject: Prayer

Hi Emma,

Hopefully you are feeling one hundred percent again. I really enjoy our discussions. As promised, I am sending you some information about what could be called the Prayer Spectrum. But first a few comments about prayer in general.

Prayer, many people would say, is talking to God. Though that's certainly true, it's a very limited description. Prayer is much more than that. In fact, you could say that any communication with God, or in which God is involved, is 'prayer'. It is not at all necessary for words to be used, whether spoken out loud or in your head. Prayer can be totally without words. In God's presence you can use your imagination, or your intuitive perception, or even aim at having no words, feelings or images at all. All of this can be called prayer. However, many people only ever pray with words. They don't practise any of the other options. That is really quite unfortunate; frequently, people don't know about the full possibilities and so their experiences of prayer and the pleasures it can bring are limited. It's a pity.

The simplest way of illustrating prayer options is by using what I call the 'Prayer Spectrum'. It looks like this. Take a sheet of paper, draw a horizontal line and write these five words above it. In the middle, write 'Worship'. On the far left, write 'Prayer Warfare'. In between, write 'Intercession'. Then on the far right write 'Contemplation', and between that and 'Worship' write 'Meditation'. So you now have, from left to right: Prayer Warfare, Intercession, Worship, Meditation and Contemplation.

Now I'll explain the difference between those concepts, and the reason why they are arranged like that. Let's start in the middle, with Worship.

Worship

Worship can mean many things. My whole life as a Christian can be an act of worship. But for our discussion, worship is best described as an exclamation of praise to God in word and in song – like you do at church. Of course you should also worship privately, perhaps during your prayer times or even while walking on the beach. You can pray aloud, or quietly in your mind. God can be worshipped anywhere at any moment, and you are encouraged to do just that. It brings strength to the soul.

As you spend time with God in adoration, you may of course like to discuss your problems, your plans or your requests; whatever bothers or excites you. That also may be categorised as worship. The Bible gives many examples of worship activities among God's people. But you would be aware of that.

Intercession

Those who intercede, present prayers of petition. Some Christians have a real gift in this area and feel called to spend a great deal of time in prayer on behalf of others, or for world situations. Intercession is based on the idea that focused, persistent prayer will help to make changes for the better. It demands considerable effort; and, although every believer at times will have a period in which this prayer becomes particularly attractive when facing problems or issues, those who consistently engage with it are few in number. It is a much-needed and valid way of praying.

Prayer Warfare

This is based on the realisation that the church is facing serious spiritual opposition in the heavenly realms. Although that opposition has been defeated on the Cross by Jesus Christ, the full outcome of this victory is historically still in the making. Some of the benefits of this victory, however, can be realised right now. Whether they are for individual believers, geographical areas or whole countries, makes no difference. God rules the whole world. Prayer warfare connects with that, and endeavours to rule by using strongly authoritative prayers that speak out against the spiritual enemy. At the same time the desired positive changes sought in prayer are being proclaimed as actually happening. God spoke things into being, the Bible tells us. Likewise, spiritual warfare prayers can be spoken out with faith and conviction making things happen against an enemy that wishes to block and destroy. That is the essence of prayer warfare. It is best done in a group, but may be undertaken individually. It has its spiritual dangers, and should not be practised without a lot of thought.

Moving along the horizontal line from Worship, through Intercession to Prayer Warfare, you will find that the energy needed for prayer increases with every step. Prayer Warfare is more demanding than Intercession, which is harder work than Worship. What makes Prayer Warfare the most demanding is that you will have to apply yourself spiritually, with faith and force, so that you can pray with conviction and a felt authority. That is no easy task. In the Prayer Spectrum, it is Prayer Warfare that greatly involves you as a person. With God, you are speaking out on behalf of God. It is individualistic; it actualises the self in prayer more than any of the other methods. But that does not make it better than the others. All are equal and have their own specific purposes.

Now let's consider the right side of the spectrum. Here, as you will see, your personal self progressively becomes quieter and less involved.

Meditation

Sometimes the words 'meditation' and 'contemplation' are used interchangeably. That's unfortunate, because they are different from each other. Contemplation is actually a progression from meditation. Meditation might be described as 'seeking enlightenment through a purposeful and reflective focus on an object, communication or imagination'. A person seeking meditation will find a place, preferably without distractions, and calmly begin to come to rest. That means rest in body, soul and spirit. It is not easy to quieten emotions and thoughts and bodily distractions, but with practice and some guidance, it can be done. 'Centring prayer' is often used – but we will talk about that at some other time, if you like.

Once reasonably at rest the person selects an object, concept, thought or idea, as central to the meditation. The possibilities are endless, though of course you would select something that you consider meaningful. Once in prayer, you approach the focus of the meditation by reflecting on it and by using your imagination. That means, you calmly let your thought processes or imagination evolve in a relaxed way. Make sure that there is never any hurry in the engagement. You can mull over some verses of Scripture, or a poem – or, if you reflect on a story, you can imagine that you are in the story and what it would look and feel like to be there. If you are meditating in a natural environment, you may wish to listen to your environment and let it happen to you.

It all requires attentiveness and a measure of internal concentration. What makes meditation so attractive is that perceptions and understandings can come about intuitively without you in any way initiating them. Without meditation, they would have passed you by.

At some point in your meditation you may also find that you are no longer working at actively imagining or reflecting, but rather that you just seem to 'be' in mediation without having to 'do' anything. When you enter this 'simply dwelling' stage, you are actually beginning to move into the realm of contemplation. Entering these modes of being requires a considerable concentration of soul and spirit, for it is not easy to remain focused and at rest. However, it is a skill that can be developed.

I must stress at this point that Christian meditation – or contemplation, for that matter – takes place with God personally being involved in the whole process. So everything happens under divine protection. It is the Spirit of God who will initiate much of the meditative process. The fear that 'the devil will sneak in to lead astray' is unfounded. If anything untoward should happen (which is possible, because of our own sinful tendencies), we can trust God to give us a clear warning. For instance, if during meditation I begin to conclude that I am superior to others, then that is pride speaking and I am clearly on the wrong track. It is then a matter of immediately cutting the meditation short and bringing the issue humbly before God, asking for help.

Contemplation

The essence of contemplation is 'unknowing' and thus by nature it is 'apophatic'. That means that contemplation arrives at its goal by purposefully discarding all words, images and whatever the senses may present. It can best be described as 'a calm dwelling upon God without word, thought or image', which may bring experiences and insights about the Source of all life that normally remain beyond human perception. The main aim of contemplation is to be with God in worship, by an act of 'simply being' that is not self-conscious.

You might want some further explanation of this. Let me try. I mentioned earlier that a meditative process might become contemplative when it begins to lose the awareness of self and stops conscious personal activity. Once you are accomplished in meditation, this can happen on a more regular basis. But there is also the possibility of deciding to skip the meditative process altogether, and start with contemplation right away. In that case, you would aim from the outset to have a mind that tries to avoid words and images. Your single desire would be one of coming to rest in order to reach a state of 'simply being' with God and a 'gazing in the Spirit', that is without cognitive processes. That may not be achieved easily; but, like meditation, it can be learned.

The experience has great benefits, even if it's hard to explain exactly what they are. It can differ each time, for God knows us and relates to us according to our own personal needs at that moment, and as God sees fit. And remember that even when seemingly nothing happens, the prayer engagement is still of significant value. Never trust your feelings in deciding how profitable or unprofitable an interaction with God may have been.

Now something about the hidden side of God, for it is true that much about God's realm remains impossible for human beings to understand. It's also true that through contemplation, what cannot normally be understood may perhaps be in part revealed. During contemplation a profound understanding may take place that literally is quite outside of this world. Such experiences can be life-changing. The contemplative may have a sudden insight that blows the mind, in that it cannot be adequately comprehended intellectually. But still it is known. When that occurs, the problem is of explaining something that was understood spiritually and quite apart from normal cognitive and intuitive processes. Everyday words no longer suffice to describe what has happened. The person will actually be lost for words. It is a situation faced by many contemplatives who have tried to record their experiences.

One thing is certain, though. Their outlook on life and the understanding of self, changes greatly because of the experience. Life becomes more significant and meaningful. That can also happen during meditation, but in contemplation it is different and more other-worldly.

Contemplation is a little like prophecy. Anyone can prophesy, but few have the office of a prophet. Likewise, contemplation as a prayer method is open to all and is to be encouraged, but few are called to become real contemplatives like the many mystics in church history. But in either situation, it is impossible to practise contemplation effectively without God's help. An involvement in this kind of prayer is initiated and assisted by God's Spirit, who operates on the principle that unless a seed dies in the ground it shall not live. When undertaken properly, both meditation and contemplation are processes of negation that lead to liberation and healing. The death of our troublesome self will release the life of our deeper self, which is the true self we have in Jesus Christ. It is obvious how important this is; ideally, every Christian should be able to practise meditation regularly, and possibly also contemplation, for it brings strength and wholeness to life in a busy and uncertain world.

In conclusion it might be helpful to consider the story of Elijah that is recorded in 1 Kings 17 – 19. It begins with his quiet preparation at the brook of Kedron, which eventually brings him to a powerful confrontation with the opposition, the false prophets of Baal, at Mount Carmel. Elijah is victorious in this spiritual warfare, but soon afterwards he falls into a state of exhaustion and suicidal depression. God cares, and lifts him up. Elijah is guided to a quiet place. After a period of separation he has the ability to listen to the still small voice, which is what God intended.

We all need that still small voice regularly speaking to us. It is a good example of how times of action need to be supported by reflection and quieter moments in the Christian life.

That's it, Emma. It's far too brief really. But at least it will give you an overview. Hope you're doing OK – and I look forward to meeting again.

Blessings,

Joe

6

Presence, Places and Silences

'It wasn't anything super-dynamic,' Emma said to Joe, 'but there was a real presence.'

Her housemates had all been away one evening, and Emma had felt moved to practise meditation. After her last discussion with Joe, and reading some of her notes, she identified with much of what he had said. Also, deep down she recognised a kind of inner prompting that she should not ignore.

'It's rather amazing. A Bible verse came into my mind, about there being many places in God's house. I looked it up and read it slowly a few times, sitting on my bed. That was when I felt a really solid and kindly mood come into my room. It added itself to the quiet music I was playing. Once that mood came, I stopped reading and just sat there – I don't know for how long. All I sensed was that I was OK, and that I would make it through OK. It was an amazing feeling, very positive and clean. After a while I fell back on my bed. For some reason I tried to stop thinking – perhaps I was remembering that e-mail you sent me. Even that worked for a while. I was just there, with this presence. I can't really describe it. Then I began to pray in my mind; and suddenly what I had known all along became an absolute certainty. The presence was Jesus.'

Joe allowed the pause to continue.

'I hope that doesn't sound over the top,' added Emma as an afterthought. She was still coming to grips with what had happened. The meditative experience had been powerful and encouraging, but she was wrestling with her perceptions of Christianity. Years ago, with good reason, she had concluded that Christianity was a nice support system for those who couldn't handle the real world.

'No, it doesn't.'

'It felt really solid,' she explained.

'It would have been,' Joe agreed. 'Christianity can require quite a bit of courage. There's nothing weak about genuine Christian experiences.'

'No – I didn't think there was,' Emma said. Whatever Jesus had conveyed to her, it had been comforting; but it was also challenging, and difficult to put into words.

'You've had quite a meditation,' said Joe. 'Not something I expected, although there's no reason why it shouldn't have happened.'

They were drinking coffee again, but this time indoors: the weather was wet and windy.

'It's interesting that your main feeling was one of being OK,' Joe observed. 'What was it like?'

'It was just a feeling. It seemed to be telling me that I am OK; not perfect, just quite OK. I felt somehow convinced that there is a place for me. Not in heaven – though I suppose it's there as well – but in life. But don't ask me how it told me.'

'There *is* a place for you, and it's very important that you have realised it! Paul Tournier, a medical doctor who was a fine Christian and knew a lot about psychology, once wrote that many people have considerable difficulty in finding their place. If they do not have a real sense of belonging in their childhood home, they will struggle when they become adults to achieve the necessary internal security that they need if they are to go out into the world and establish a place. I'm not talking about buying a house. It's about identity, about being strong enough in your own right and feeling that you are. It is psychological, and it's spiritual, but it's true enough. We all need to feel that we belong.'

'That's the kind of thing I felt. A sense of belonging.'

'Keep reminding yourself of it! Belonging is a most necessary feeling in life. It has all sorts of benefits, such as self-acceptance. However – and this is important – you cannot create a place of belonging off your own bat. It needs to be given by other people. It starts during childhood with family members, and if things aren't right then, you are likely to experience identity and security troubles later.'

Emma thought of home. It hadn't been too bad, but not always too good either. She was struck again by how well Joe seemed to understand things. Maybe he had had his own struggles, or simply knew about people by what he had seen and read.

'Your meditation was quite significant,' Joe concluded, 'and you may wish to reflect on it further in future. Make sure particularly that you are always affirming that special sense of "OK" in your mind. Don't lose touch with it. Let nothing take it away, particularly not your own thinking, the negative thoughts you may get about yourself.'

'I do get those sometimes,' Emma admitted.

'Of course you do. Everybody does. Some more than others. It's a matter of the right self-acceptance. It's not easy to accept yourself. That's where spending time in the presence of God can be so beneficial. It reveals you to yourself, with the help of One who knows you better than you do, and is kind about it. You'll learn that you're not that terrific – and that you don't have to be. Just "good enough" will do. You will become kinder on yourself as well. You'll find that you have a need to grow as a person;

and God can help with this.' Joe paused, and wondered whether he was perhaps presenting this information rather too concisely.

'So Christianity is much more than just going to church and behaving properly,' said Emma. That appealed to her. She knew from past experience that there had to be more, but nobody had ever explained it to her.

'Exactly! It goes far deeper, and it's much more exciting,' Joe agreed. 'It concerns itself with me, as a person – in my very being. "To be OK" comes first, and then "to *do* OK". Christianity shows you who you are, and how you can become more of an integrated person. Few people realise this, not even most Christians. It's a pity.'

'So God can help.'

'The best help,' Joe agreed. 'He knows what needs adjusting in our lives. He will progressively undo all the damaging messages that have come our way. It's a liberating experience.' Joe decided to add one final suggestion. 'Spiritual practices are central to the process of self-discovery – at least, if you want to work at it effectively.'

Emma opened her notebook and picked up a pen. 'Go over the main points again,' she said.

Joe bought orange juice for each of them. Coffee was a fine stimulant, but he needed something fresher on his palate. Emma showed no sign of wanting to stop the discussion.

'Did you actually set out to practise solitude, or did the meditation work without it?' Joe asked.

'I didn't do anything deliberately about solitude. But after the meditation I looked it up in my notes. I'm a pretty busy person. It's hard to get my head round the idea.'

'I find it hard too,' Joe admitted. 'Every week I have to remind myself to take it seriously. Being an active person tempts you to be busy all the time. It can be a real trap.'

'So what can one do about it?'

'Luckily solitude isn't the only reality we can seek. There's another – silence. Solitude and silence are complementary. They help each other.'

Emma sipped her juice.

'If you find it difficult to practise solitude, you can start by aiming at silence. For example, I might stop using words so excessively, in so many ways. There are just too many words in life – unless one does something about it. Do you remember I mentioned Henri Nouwen last time? He warns us that words have crowded into our lives so much that they often stop communicating anything meaningful. The overkill of words has stopped us from properly connecting with their content. So we are confronted with many words, but they can be quite meaningless.'

Joe was warming to his theme. 'Just think about it! Wherever I look, I can see words! And I speak words myself, lots of words, every day. Then there is what I'm thinking – another multitude of words. The mind boggles! And actually my mind often *does* feel the strain. Words are everywhere. What's the solution? I have to restrict the number of words that crowd into my space every day. It can be done. It's difficult, of course. I can't very well stop talking altogether when I am with people, and I can't easily shut my mind down. But I can try to for specific periods. And that's the key.'

'You mean you just stop talking for a while?'

'Yes. And I try to limit the use of words in my thinking.'

'How can you do that?'

'Not easily,' Joe conceded. 'Let's look at talking first. If you were to analyse how many inessential words you say every day, you'd be surprised. For instance, being sociable with people can mean a lot of talk that is only of secondary importance, though it is necessary for relational purposes. However, for certain periods every week, such talking could be minimised so that you can distance yourself from all that verbosity. Actually, you can often avoid social chat without being too obvious about it.'

Emma was absorbed, her chin propped on her hands, her juice left unfinished. Outside, the rain drummed gently against the window.

'Many words come to us through radio and TV. Do we really need to hear all that is on offer? It usually makes very little difference to our lives. It's information overload! That influence can be reduced as well. Think how much more restful your day would become if you switched off the radio and TV – particularly if you could slow the words in your mind down as well.'

'And how would I do that?' Emma was curious to know the answer. She often caught herself thinking excessively.

'Good question,' Joe acknowledged. 'How can I put it best? You can do it, but it is difficult. For a start, you could direct your thoughts to one thing of worth, rather than to a thousand things of little value. Our thoughts tend to take charge: we have to wrest back control. A large part of our environment is designed to infiltrate our thinking and take over our minds. Think about advertising hoardings, for example. There's a battle for what controls your mind.'

It was raining hard now. The coffee shop was packed with damp refugees from the downpour. Joe and Emma's table was in a corner, away from the main hubbub. Emma had no difficulty in hearing Joe's thoughtful explanations, even in the middle of the noisy coffee shop.

'If I asked you to focus your thoughts lightly on an image, perhaps some art that you're fond of, could you do it?' continued Joe. 'I'm not saying think deeply about it, just keep it central in your awareness.'

'I think I could do that.'

'And if I asked you to refuse to let your mind drift into pointless deliberations, but to think only about what was immediately relevant, could you do that?'

'I could probably manage that too. But maybe only in short spells.'

'Now then: let's combine the two. So you'll think when it is really necessary, but you'll be ready to switch to the art image at other times. You'll try not to get caught in other modes of thinking that are not immediately essential. Ideally, reflecting on the image should not involve words – just letting it dwell in your mind, quietly, as a focus. If you were to do all that, you would have reduced considerably the words moving around in your head every day.'

'Might be possible,' Emma conceded. 'But it won't be easy.'

'It gets easier the more you get used to doing it,' Joe said. 'Again – it's a skill that can be learned. Personally, I usually try to dwell on God's presence as a focus. Of course you don't have to choose art. You can choose whatever you like, so long as it is significant and comfortable. Perhaps you should try this exercise.'

'I might do that,' said Emma.

'The practice of silence is an obvious help towards solitude – to being with yourself in a meaningful way,' Joe concluded. He produced a small package from his pocket and handed it to Emma.

'I brought you a small present,' he explained. 'It's a CD you might like. It's Gregorian Chant. I could tell you a lot about that kind of music, but not right now. See if you enjoy it. It can be helpful for slowing down, and as a background to meditation. That CD became very popular a few years ago. Lots of young people bought it. Anyway, see how you go.'

'Thanks, Joe. I'll certainly listen to it.'

'And Emma – one last thing. If, the next time you meditate, nothing significant seems to happen, don't be disappointed. Being with God is always meaningful. Even if sometimes, it doesn't feel that way.'

7

Holy Leisure

Joe was frustrated. He had lots to do and was finding it increasingly difficult not to let his irritation get the upper hand. It probably already had. That shouldn't happen; not when you were the one giving out all the advice on how irritation might be avoided. But it does happen, he reflected, and would do so again. You have to struggle for your sanity. That was one of his pet phrases. At least it wasn't a lost cause.

What he needed was a day of holy leisure. A few days, in fact. The old monastic concept of never running, never standing still; slowly moving forward with all your attention focused on the present moment and whatever it required. Don't think of what is ahead, or what has passed. Give all your attention to the task at hand. Take time to smell the flowers, some would say. That is, if like the monks of old, you would walk the paths between the church and the dormitory. 'Or in my case our college garden,' Joe thought. In that way, by slowing things down, you could get back control of your circumstances and bring some balance and rest into your daily life.

'Taking off the pace and being properly focused is not what I am doing right now,' Joe concluded. On many issues his thoughts were miles ahead, while what presently kept him busy got only half the attention it deserved.

He had an unfocused mind, his feelings were edgy, and he was tired. Something deep down was bothering him as well, but he couldn't quite figure out what. 'So much for the benefits of spiritual exercises,' Joe thought. Which was unfair, for it was the very lack of these exercises recently that had placed him in his present position. Tomorrow simply had to be a holy leisure day.

He mapped it out in his mind. Tonight, home from work, he would first do a few stretches to get some tension out of his body. Then he would lie on his back relaxing with choral music playing: a Mass, perhaps, or a Russian choir singing spiritual songs. It would take time for his system to slow down, but it would work out fine. Everybody ideally ought to have a way of slowing down quickly and effectively. Different people did it different ways, but at the centre of the exercise was a reduction in bodily tensions, emotional pressure and random thought patterns. Once lying still, Joe knew, his body would at first urge him to make movements; but he could resist that. Maybe some slight movement, early on, to release muscular pressure might be necessary. But that should settle down, and then his breathing would become regular, and he would be able to let the music help him to relax.

A potential problem was Joe's habit of analysing music to which he was listening – something definitely to be avoided in this exercise. That was why he sometimes played music by Messiaen, whose keyboard pieces had no clear melody lines or orchestral arrangements. Analysis was the opposite of what his mind should be busy with. Nor should he rationalise his feelings, or worry about them. He should drop all that and become properly still, with his spirit directed towards God: just being in God's presence. Of course thoughts would drop in, but he need not engage with them. Just let the thoughts drift in, and by being left alone, drift out. By relaxing in this way he could begin to undo the tensions of an overly busy life-style and have a greater sense of God's presence.

Sometimes that kind of relaxation worked very well, and it was beautiful. At other times he was less successful. But it was always worthwhile, even if he fell asleep, which had happened more than once. 'Take it as it comes,' Joe would say, 'and forget setting any goals with it. After all it's not meant to be a challenge, quite the opposite. You're supposed to relax and stop worrying.'

And tomorrow? That was going to be a holy leisure day. It meant that he would get out of bed slowly, take a shower slowly, and eat breakfast slowly. He would feel the carpet under his bare feet, and the water on his skin, and he would taste his food instead of just eating it. And all that, at a reduced pace. Then, don't get irritated with the traffic, go with the flow. Make sure not to think of work until arriving behind the desk but rather consider the Lord. Once busy it would be a matter of working steadily, one job at a time, no wasting of energy; and allowing for brief periods of reflection or mental prayer.

Above all, Joe warned himself, don't get animated with problems or opportunities. Keep a distance emotionally from the good and the bad that always come your way during a day in the office. The idea would be to keep things on an even keel, minimise unnecessary talk, and make sure to have a leisurely lunch.

Joe knew what such a day should feel like. He would achieve no less than during any other day, but he would be less weary doing so. He would feel more in control, able to face pressure with a cool head. He would set the day to his hand, rather than the day dictating to him. Creativity would flow and a good laugh was likely; 'Never take yourself too seriously' was good advice. Joe began to look forward to a holy leisure day tomorrow.

So why wasn't every day like that? 'Because our natural tendencies have a powerful pull in the opposite direction,' Joe concluded. It was unfortunate, but true. You had indeed to fight for your sanity.

Of course it wasn't all a struggle. Life had many good moments without holy leisure days. Really, the overriding question, for everybody actually, was how to get the most out of being alive, and how to make best sense of it? Joe had found his answers in becoming a Christian. Or, more precisely, through that special connectedness he now felt with God, or Jesus – which was the same anyway. He remembered when he had searched for a foundation stone that seemed to be missing from his perceptions of reality. The existential picture had felt incomplete, and the world a place with too many unanswered questions. That was years ago now.

These days many of those questions still remained without satisfactory answers. But having experienced some of the underlying spiritual reality behind the universe, that wasn't such an issue any more. Although, to be honest, Joe thought the world rather a mess. He felt sad about that and in response tried to do some good in places. However, he wasn't Superman, and could only help just a little in the huge tapestry of human life and nature. He probably didn't do enough.

It was difficult, and a constant challenge, to know where to draw the line in helping others and taking up good causes. Joe lost no sleep over that. But he knew he shouldn't ignore the problem either, and that could happen all too easily.

Joe felt loved and accepted, and therefore able to deal with a multitude of matters in life without experiencing destructive thoughts about himself as a person. He wasn't all that terrific, didn't want to be, and felt no need to be.

Some years ago, during meditation, Joe had for a moment seen the veil lifted from the love-dynamic, God's nature, that exists behind the universe. It had been wonderfully overpowering and indescribable to discover that universal love. It is reflected in human love, but is ever so much deeper and stronger. From then on Joe had been happy to remain agnostic in life about many matters. He possessed a certainty now that this divine love, only partially revealed to him, would make all things well eternally. It was what Julian of Norwich, an anchoress in medieval England, wrote after seeing a vision of Jesus Christ: that 'All will be well, and all manner of things shall be well.' It was a comforting realisation, onto which a person could only hold by faith in God – in Joe's case that faith was helped by his revelatory experience of love. Why he had been granted that fortunate moment of insight, Joe didn't know, but it was definitely not because of personal merit.

These days there is much written theologically about the love and acceptance of God towards all people, Joe reflected. Christians are the ones to accept that love, but in reality many find coming to grips with it as a personal experience difficult. Often believers could subscribe to the idea of a loving God, but had no idea what it should feel like. God might love them, but that didn't translate into anything distinctly emotional – which was fair enough, Joe conceded. The daily experience of God's love was subtler than that. It was more a sure sense of being positively known, accepted and supported unconditionally.

Such spiritual awareness, however, would not come without a continual personal response to God's invitation. You had to say 'Yes' to God all the time and mean it. Accepting the truth of God's love in principle and

experiencing its reality were two different matters altogether. Cognitive assent would not automatically translate into felt experience.

It was indeed necessary to say 'Yes' to the divine invitation
initially and then find ways of staying in touch with God –
like prayer, reflection and reading. This needed to be done
with the heart and not just the head, as connecting with
God is in essence a relational activity: God is relational
and can only be personally known in that way.

There is never the slightest accusation or rejection in
God's love, Joe mused, and never will be. But often people
cannot readily accept that. Somehow, because of life's conditioning, many who seek God bring a measuring rod to
the holy encounter and decide secretly that they fall short
of the minimum requirements. They bring their self-
perceptions of what God thinks about them into the equa-
tion. It's understandable, but it puts the cart before the
horse. If God has accepted unconditionally, it is not for
humans to begin introducing standards.

For Christian there are, of course, standards to live up
to. But that is an attitudinal matter, quite different from
God's all-embracing love. Love comes first, and completely accepts you, and then encourages you to do well.
'Being accepted' comes before 'Doing OK'.

'Otherwise there's a real danger of simply having a
cause-and-effect kind of faith, in which everything comes
back to the question of whether I do well enough,' Joe
thought. He had long got past that point, and was determined never again to fall back into it.

Yet, he accepted, the concept of unconditional love is not
something that can be grasped easily. It needs to be
revealed to a person and become firmly anchored in the
soul.

These revelations are freely given, reflected Joe, to anyone who is willing to become spiritually relational with God. But not everyone takes up that offer; and many Christians have limited experience of God's love. It is a matter of prayer and spiritual exercises, otherwise faith will remain a mostly mental belief only and will not last the distance.

'Getting the best out of life is not easy,' Joe thought. Sorting it all can be confusing. Personally, he had resolved the puzzle of life enough to live with a measure of certainty. Some insights seemed clear to him now and formed the basis of his beliefs.

The first was that God had invited him to experience divine love and care, and that it would follow him right into eternity. That didn't guarantee an earthly life without problems and grief, but they belonged to the stuff of life – no more, no less.

Secondly, to live well you needed to be part of a cause much larger than yourself. In a sense, you had to sign your life away to that. Only then could real purpose and meaning be found. To Joe, that cause was his faith in Jesus Christ; and he could not ask for better.

Finally, Joe had concluded that life was never simple and that it was pointless to ask why many things happened the way they did. The answer to life is not found by finding reasons for everything, but by living in relationship with God and other people in spite of everything.

'A little simplistic perhaps,' Joe thought, 'but if it wasn't simple I couldn't possibly live by it. And being simple doesn't make it less true.'

He was tired. He really needed that day of holy leisure tomorrow.

8

The Dream

The bus was travelling at the speed limit. Through the window, Emma looked out at open country full of red earth. She was on the way back to the city from a few days at her family home on a trip she could well have done without – she had been attending a funeral. Gazing towards the horizon she saw little of the scenery. Her mind was elsewhere. Not surprisingly, she was feeling exhausted and depressed.

She'd got the news one morning a few days ago: James had died in a car accident on a country road in the early hours. Drink and driving wasn't a good mix. Emma had known James since their high school days, but hadn't seen much of him in recent years. He was related to one of Emma's aunts. His death was a community tragedy, and Emma had decided to make the five-hour journey home.

For a few months, back in high school, she and James had been an item. Typical teenage stuff, Emma mused. But it had been James who had given her her first real kiss, the kind that leaves you confused and excited. Now he was dead, killed in an instant, wasted in seconds, a total mess of a situation. The funeral had been controlled and digni-fied, but there was an underlying sense of deep tragedy. I'm too young to have friends die on me, Emma thought. Last year, another friend had committed suicide. Life doesn't think you're ever too young for anything, she told herself. Tears began to well up. She wiped them away with the back of her hand.

The bus did not have many passengers. Emma had two seats to herself. She felt like stretching across both for a sleep but decided it would be too uncomfortable. There wasn't much point in reading her book, either: she couldn't concentrate and wasn't that interested in the story. Traffic was minimal. The bus was travelling alone through a vast landscape: an object passing through as fast as possible, an unnatural intrusion into an alien environment. Just how I feel, Emma reflected. She felt lonely and out of place, between destinations. It was strangely painful. There'd been too much sorrow during these last few days, she concluded.

She often felt alone, as if she were unknown to other people, even her friends, and could only connect with them superficially. Her mother was forever wondering when she would get a bloke; but that could wait. She wanted to travel first, and then if the right guy came along she might possibly start a relationship. Having grown up with two brothers, she wasn't impatient to hook up with the male of the species particularly quickly.

She suspected that her feelings of loneliness and being unknown were an existential reality common to all human beings, something you can't escape from. That didn't make it any easier, though. Today, because she was depressed, it was hitting her harder. She'd get over it, keep the feeling at bay, and manage. Emma knew herself to be a fighter. She had decided years ago, at a point in her life that called for some definite responses, that you either fight for your existence or you hand the best part of your life over to external forces. She was prepared to do battle. It seemed the right response, but it left her with a sense of loss all the same. The bus began slowing down for a stop in a small country town.

Going home had been all right. But she was long past the stage where it was the main location of her life. It was home – but she didn't live there. A few days, in fact, had been long enough. As usual there had been too many tensions and dynamics going on. Nothing bad, just normal family stuff, but she had moved on from that. In a way that was sad; Emma had a sense of loss about what could have been. Not that she had any idea what exactly it was that she might have missed out on; it was just a feeling.

Her mother, as always, had been glad to see her, all the more because her visit was unexpected. She had simply arrived. If she had been asked why she arrived unannounced, she would have been unable to explain it. Was she getting her own back for something, or perhaps enforcing her independence? Or had she just wanted to surprise her mother? Emma didn't know and would rather not find out. Her mother was a good person, and they didn't argue any more. It was nice to notice the pleasure she took from Emma's achievements at university. But all was not well between them. Emma suspected that her mother was patiently waiting for things to change, perhaps in future. She hoped for that too, and she thought it could happen. But right now there was little she could do about her feelings.

She was the first family member to leave home – apart from her dad of course, currently sailing somewhere in Indonesia. Her mother missed her, Emma knew, and occasionally made pointed (though understandable) comments about her infrequent visits. Nevertheless, when Emma had climbed on board the bus three hours ago she had done so with little regret. Maybe she should have felt sad, but she hadn't. And that itself was sad, in a way. 'This funeral is making a real mess of me,' she thought. Issues that were normally concealed were crowding in on her.

Last night she'd had a dream. She had been walking alone through a deserted valley white with snow, and not a footprint in sight except her own. It was a calm day. The valley was shadowed, with hills on both sides, and ran slightly downward. A lone wolf was stalking her relentlessly, following from a distance on the horizon behind her. It was ominous but not an immediate threat, like a shadow that might pounce one day. 'I wasn't afraid,' Emma remembered, 'but I wasn't at ease either.' She wanted urgently to get away from the wolf. Walking more quickly made no difference, for the wolf moved faster in turn. Once it stopped and howled, an eerie cry thrown into empty space. She shivered. An unmistakeable dread crept up on her. Apart from the wolf's cry, the valley was peaceful. Emma knew this peace to be an illusion. It was a place you could easily get lost in, and she probably would. The wolf in the distance never let up.

She needed desperately to get out of the valley. She didn't know if she could, or even if she wanted to enough. She knew she should escape – but would she? Escaping would be a matter of simply walking up the hillside, over the top and out of the valley. The wolf belonged to the valley and would not follow. Its very bearing threatened to stop her, but she knew, with that absolute knowledge that one only has in dreams, that wolf could not withstand a challenge. It would be a challenge of wills – hers against the wolf's.

The wolf, though menacing, had something familiar about it, something they shared, as if in a sense they were feeding off each other. It wasn't a good situation to be in. Emma knew she had to get out of the valley and out of the shade. The climb uphill would take determination, and she could only make a start when she had committed herself to that course of action. Emma needed to decide, and to set her mind with complete conviction. Otherwise there would be no escape from the wolf and this deceptive valley.

Emma understood her dream quite well. The invitation in it had actually been stronger than the threat.

She looked out the window of the bus, which was now travelling through vineyard country. It was autumn. The leaves on the vines had turned red; her artist's eye momentarily became enchanted with the wonderful world of colour around her. One day she would come back here for some serious work. But first, she would go overseas. That was a definite bright prospect on the horizon.

She briefly wondered if the wolf would follow her there. Of course it would, if she let it. It wasn't a comforting thought. She should do something about it properly, quite soon. But not when you're depressed, Emma told herself. It's never any good making major decisions when you're down. That was true enough, though it felt like a cop-out. Her depression was turning into an irritation, one she should get out of. 'Once the bus arrives in the city', she promised herself.

During the last few days she had tried to pray. It hadn't worked. How can a senseless accident ever lead to helpful prayer – unless maybe you were a saint? But there lay the rub. The world abounded with senseless and abhorrent events. If that became a legitimate barrier to prayer, you never would pray. Emma felt that the answers to life were not to be found in trying to make sense of the world. Nobody could; she was convinced of that, even if some people thought they'd got it sorted. Instead you needed to seek communication with God. That was difficult, and especially so if you didn't pray regularly.

'I'm still in the valley,' Emma reflected. The wolf was still stalking her, and she was walking mostly downhill. 'Once I decide to turn,' Emma thought, 'it will be for good.' Perhaps that was why she wasn't going to turn right now. Doing it properly seemed a costly decision. But was that really so? There was a price to pay, but the benefits would be much greater.

'I'm OK,' Emma thought, with some relief. And now she remembered her meditation, that special one with so much positive content and encouragement. In a way it was history now. The memory had faded, yet it stayed with her as a promise. It was about the other side of the hill, out of the valley. That much was obvious.

Emma had decided that the dream came from God. Perhaps it was an answer to her recent feeble attempts at prayer. But why was it so difficult to acknowledge with gratitude where the dream came from? It was a spiritual dream about spiritual matters. Perhaps it was the wolf that kept her back, which was of a different spirit altogether.

The bus was entering the city. It would be at the Bus Station in twenty minutes.

Before she had left, Emma had warned Joe that she would be unable to keep their next appointment because of the funeral. She had promised to ring him on her return. Now she decided, as the city streets glided by, that she really should make up her mind properly about God before contacting Joe. She was still stalling and she knew it. Somewhere the wolf howled another of its eerie cries.

Centring Prayer and Spiritual Reading

It was a month after Emma's visit home. Soon after getting back, she had received an e-mail from Joe, asking how she was getting on. She'd sent a brief reply and left it at that. Joe was worried about her, but decided that she needed space. Eventually she phoned him, partly because it seemed good manners, and partly because she needed to talk. It seemed as if she had lost focus and the rhythm had gone out of her life.

'It's good to hear from you, Emma. I'm glad you phoned. Yes, of course I'd be delighted to meet up.' Her voice at the other end of the line sounded very depressed. He made a decision. 'Why don't we meet here, at my home? We could talk for longer, in comfort.'

There was a long pause. Joe suddenly realised how his invitation might be misconstrued. 'You could come next Tuesday. My wife will be here then. She'd love to meet you.'

'I'd love to come,' said Emma.

Joe's home was a pleasant house in a quiet street not far from the university; nothing special, but comfortable. Emma had found it easily. Joe's wife Jane, a pleasant relaxed woman, welcomed her and took her through to the study.

'Hi, Emma. It's nice to see you again. How was the funeral?'

'Not good – but I managed.' Emma kept her deeper thoughts, about the death of friends and her return home, to herself. Joe didn't probe further.

'And how are you feeling generally – still OK?'

'No,' Emma admitted, 'I feel terrible.'

Joe nodded sympathetically. 'It happens,' he said.

'I feel as if I've lost control. Everything is taking over.'

That was about as brief as it could get, Emma thought, but she couldn't be bothered with the details. She was struggling with an overwhelming feeling that events and emotions were overtaking her, that she was not doing the living from her own centre. It was very frustrating; it must not continue; she needed answers, someone to turn to. Fortunately, there was Joe.

'I know how you're feeling,' said Joe. 'Life brings all sorts of situations, opportunities and challenges, and it's not easy to stay on top of it all.'

'You're right. Everything seems to have got on top of me these days.'

'Your rhythm has been disrupted.'

'Yes.' Emma took some comfort from Joe's understanding.

'Could you give me a reason why it's happening?' asked Joe.

'It's not one big thing. It's lots of small things. They all add to the problem. College assignments. Extra shifts at work. And my housemates are really noisy right now. I guess I'm just exhausted. Sometimes I could just burst into tears.'

She wondered if she should have said that, but Joe made no comment. He could see that Emma was quite close to tears at that moment.

*

'I hope you like walnut cake!'

Jane appeared in the doorway with a tray loaded with coffee and cake. 'I've got cold fruit juice in the fridge if you'd rather,' she said. A cold drink sounded attractive. 'I'd love a fruit juice,' Emma smiled.

While Jane was away Emma surveyed the room in more detail. There were books everywhere, family photographs arranged on the window sills, a framed seascape on the wall and a desk with a computer almost covered with papers. She looked again at the seascape with an artist's critical eye and decided that she approved. The room seemed much used and there was clear evidence of creativity. Joe was obviously not a person who took things easy.

Jane returned with the juice, and left. Joe poured himself a cup of coffee. 'You know,' he said gently, 'I realise exactly how you feel. I struggle myself quite a lot with the downside of being often busy. There are answers, and we'll talk about them. But don't think I've got myself all sorted out. It's not easy to maintain a good balance of spirit and soul while having an active lifestyle. Have some cake,' he added, passing her a plate.

'The first step is to recognise when matters are getting out of hand. Then you can make adjustments, for the problems won't disappear automatically. Usually it isn't one particular adjustment that you have to make – many factors play a part in maintaining the necessary balance. Some are very practical and obvious, but still easily neglected: like, for instance the question of sleep. What has your sleep pattern been like lately?' Joe asked.

'Not great,' she admitted.

'So you need to sort that out for a start.'

'I could have a hot bath,' Emma suggested. She liked baths, though sometimes resented the time they took. 'Baths are relaxing.'

'Yes, or you could do some stretching, or make some herbal tea. But when you are really worn out, one evening of special care won't fix a poor sleeping pattern. It takes at least a few days.'

Emma could see the point Joe was making. She decided to have a bath that night.

'And then there's physical fitness. Exercise is important. It helps you cope better with the demands of daily life.'

'I play soccer every week.' Emma had joined the university team and really enjoyed the game. Playing midfield was quite demanding physically. If she were asked to play today, she probably wouldn't have the energy to do so.

'That's great. Our bodies are central to our chances of well being. Sleep and exercise are important. And watch, too, what you eat and drink – or rather, how much or how little you eat.'

Emma munched her cake thoughtfully. Jane was certainly a wonderful cook.

'Control in life is mainly a matter of your spirit finding the space and rhythm it needs,' Joe explained. 'So much puts our spirits under pressure, both from outside us and from inside. If your spirit has space to move, you're better placed to deal with life. It's a fact that has been known for thousands of years, and daily systems have been designed to facilitate such spiritual liberty. One example is the Rule of St Benedict, which has been adapted to many different situations over the centuries. You can still find it being practised in monastic orders today.'

'A "rule"?'

'Yes. It comes from a word meaning "to measure". A monastic Rule is a way of dividing the day into sections by times of prayer and worship. It includes instructions about the behaviour expected of a monk. These Rules simply allow for an assessment – a measurement, if you like – of how well the monastery is achieving its objectives, which all aim at facilitating a close relationship with God.'

Sitting back in her comfortable chair, Emma was beginning to realise how tired she really was. But she was not finding it hard to follow what Joe was saying. She just relaxed and let his voice come to her. Her mind was taking in information without much corresponding thought activity. It was quite a pleasant process.

'Obviously we're not in a monastery, and it would be impossible for us to use that system in our daily activities. But we do need at least some practices every day that will help our spirit to find space. The question is, how can we best incorporate a few spiritual disciplines into (ideally) every day; and what might those disciplines be? We've talked about some already – solitude and silence. But it's not easy.'

No, it isn't, Emma thought. In fact it seems almost impossible.

'Still,' Joe continued, 'that's the challenge. Fortunately, there are other more flexible options as well as scheduling special times into your day for prayer, reading and reflection. I'll explain one to you in a moment that you might want to use during a prayer time. Actually, you could use it at any time, and anywhere. It's called "centring prayer".'

'What does that mean?' Emma asked. It sounded like something to do with focusing.

'It sharpens your spiritual focus.'

I got that right, she thought to herself. She should know; her own focus was all over the place right now. The centre seemed to have dropped out of her life.

Joe continued. 'Centring prayer strengthens your spirit. It pulls things together and settles you down. Christians who have a charismatic background might quietly speak in other tongues to achieve it, but there are other ways.'

Emma understood the term 'speaking in tongues' from past church experience; one of her friends used to pray in that way.

'You will begin to experience more peace,' said Joe. 'You'll feel more yourself, and thus more able to deal with life. Centring prayer means using a short prayer of your own choice, over and over for a while, without stopping. You can repeat the prayer audibly or silently in your mind. Tradition teaches that ideally the prayer will begin to repeat itself automatically, in your heart. Developing a 'heart prayer' will take time. It is a gift from God, and it doesn't happen easily.'

'Like a mantra?' Emma suggested.

'It's similar, but I wouldn't call it a mantra. It's not a repetitive formula, it's more a continuous reaching out to God by means of a brief statement of intent. John Main, who founded a monastic community in Montreal that also caters for lay people, taught the word *Maranatha* as a good starting point in meditative prayer. It means "Come, Lord." You say it continuously and it helps to centre your attentions on God. Personally,' Joe added, 'I prefer the "Jesus Prayer".'

'What's that?'

'Remember I talked about the Desert Fathers and Mothers? The tradition of the Jesus Prayer goes back to them. They used centring prayer in practising solitude and silence. The Jesus Prayer is a prayer sentence attributed to them, though today it is better known through a story told in a classic of Russian folk lore, *The Way of the Pilgrim*. This anonymous book tells of a nineteenth-century pilgrim in the Russian Steppes who was seeking the meaning of "pray without ceasing". Eventually he met a *staretz* – a wise and holy man – who taught him the Jesus Prayer.

After much practice using it audibly and mentally, the pilgrim found that the prayer indeed began repeating itself in his heart automatically. This prayer, by the way, is quite central to spirituality in the Orthodox Church.'

Emma wasn't quite sure what 'Orthodox' meant but didn't ask. 'What are the words?' she asked.

'The version I prefer is the longer one: "Lord Jesus Christ, Son of God, have mercy on me, a sinner." But you can make it shorter if you wish. Some just use the words, "Jesus, have mercy." The idea is to repeat these words in rhythm with your breathing. For instance you can breathe in with the words "Lord Jesus Christ" and breathe out with "Son of God" and so on. You must always approach the prayer in a relaxed manner and then see what benefits you may experience.'

'Could I give it a try?' Emma suggested.

'Why not?' Joe agreed, 'I'll write the words out for you. Try reflecting on the meaning of the prayer while using it. It is a prayer of love, not of condemnation; so when you come to the word "sinner", do accept that you are indeed far from perfect, but God has no problems with that. Try feeling grateful for this blessing. It will increase your humility, and consequently your internal freedom. The more humble we are, the fewer hang-ups we have.'

'Lord Jesus Christ, Son of God, have mercy on me, a sinner,' Emma said softly. It felt comforting.

'The primary reason for praying this prayer is to increase your connectedness with God and also your own openness. It creates a healing dynamic and makes a person stronger. It will centre your thoughts and focus your activities. You feel more in control of things and your perspective changes. It will increase the peace of your soul. Traditionally this approach to prayer is known as "hesychasm". That means, "coming to rest".'

'So I just keep repeating it?' Emma queried.

'Yes; for a while each day, when it suits you. You can speak it out softly or in your head. Personally, I find it very helpful, and I hope you will, too.'

'I'll do that,' Emma promised. I better make sure that I do, she thought. These discussions on spirituality always left her full of good intentions, but it was easier said than done.

Joe stopped explaining for a moment and seemed to be considering something. 'I'd like you to try one more thing, if you will.'

'Sure,' Emma responded.

'Again, it's been part of the Christian tradition since the time of the Desert Fathers. It's called spiritual reading.'

Emma nodded. She was suddenly feeling really tired, and for the first time she became aware of all the other things going on: Jane in another part of the house moving something around; the clamour of birds quarrelling in the trees in next door's trim back garden; the occasional grumble of a vehicle driving along the quiet peaceful street. Hopefully Joe wasn't going to go on too much longer. Not that she didn't really appreciate his concern for her, she admonished herself.

'The Latin name is *lectio divina*,' began Joe. He felt that Emma might benefit by reading some Scripture, but in a particular way. 'I've got a printed explanation here somewhere. I'll find it in a minute.'

'Is it difficult?' Emma asked. The Latin sounded intimidating.

'Not at all. It's a very easy way of using Scripture, and it can be quite helpful.'

Emma nodded. Provided that it was easy to do, she would try it.

'Base it on a Bible passage that you find meaningful. You can start with some centring prayer – that's not part of the *lectio divina*, but it can be a helpful lead-in exercise. When you feel relaxed and spiritually focused, read the Bible verses you have selected, without hurry, and take note of what they say. It's very important that you don't hurry at any stage of this exercise.'

He finished his coffee. 'It's important, too, not to start analysing what you're reading. Think about what the verses mean, but more importantly, approach the text in a meditative fashion. Seek to taste and savour the beauty of what you read. It's a kind of discovery exercise. So, first you read, and then you reflect on it and allow the text to speak to you. How the text will respond is a spiritual dynamic that you cannot determine. Whatever the text shows you, take it on board. At the end, bring what you have learned to God in prayer. Consider too the implications of what you have discovered; how it might affect you as a person. That's it.'

Suddenly, Joe was also feeling drained. Explaining spiritual matters could be hard work.

'Thanks, Joe,' Emma said.

Joe smiled. 'You're a good person Emma. Don't give up. But a few solid sleeps are probably the most important thing you need right now.'

And a nice bath, Emma added silently, smiling back. She would play the Gregorian Chants while submerged in bubbles. She rather liked that CD.

10

Symbols, Art and Creativity

'Art is all around us,' said Joe, 'but we don't see it. Of course few of us can be called "artists", but we all have the ability to perceive and look with enlarged understanding, to see things differently – if only our spiritual disposition would let us.'

Emma was sitting with a group of Joe's students, in the lecture hall at his college. It was the first time she had heard him give a formal lecture. Today his topic was 'Spirituality, Art and Creativity', and he had asked Emma if she would like to attend. Emma was feeling quite at home in this new situation.

'Let me give you an example that might help. It's not about art, but the dynamics are similar. Who knows the difference between a sign and a symbol?'

'A sign conveys information,' one student ventured.

'Exactly, and what does a symbol do?'

'It represents something,' another suggested.

'Yes! Very good. For instance, for an Australian, a kangaroo on a traffic sign is simply a warning to drive carefully in case you hit one. The same image on the tail of a Qantas jet at New York airport might elicit feelings about home in Australia far away. You might even get homesick for a moment. Now why would that be?'

'Memories,' someone suggested.

'Yes,' Joe continued, 'there is a whole world behind that image on that plane. When the image connects you with that other world, then it has become a symbol. The symbolic is very important, for it opens up experiences which otherwise would be closed to us.' Joe was warming to his theme. 'When is the cross a sign, and when is it a symbol?' he asked.

'It's usually a symbol,' came a reply.

'No, a sign,' someone responded.

A brief discussion developed among the students. Joe allowed it to run on for a while without intervening. Emma guessed where all of this might be leading. She was enjoying herself. She had always found her experiences of modern churches symbolically limiting.

'A young man I know,' Joe continued, 'attends a church that has a huge cross up on the wall behind the pulpit. He usually just looks at it. But one Easter, for reasons he does not understand, that cross became alive to him and he was deeply affected. It changed his life. Some of the "other" world behind that cross was revealed to him. He had a symbolic experience; and at that moment, that cross went from being a sign to a symbol.

'The symbolic requires relational dynamics to take place. The problem is that we, as people, don't experience enough of this kind of relating. Also, the possibilities of symbolism are wider than just images. For instance a candle, representing light, could function as a symbol, and open up understanding.'

'My church doesn't have any signs that could become symbols,' a young woman in the group observed.

'With what consequences?' Joe asked.

'With our lively worship, we don't need symbols to get in contact with God,' one student suggested.

'No, of course not,' Joe agreed, 'I can accept that. But does that make the symbolic obsolete?'

'In a modern church I suppose that would be the case,' the same student responded.

'We should have both,' someone else concluded. 'There is no reason why the symbolic shouldn't be important.'

'It depends on who you are as a person, too,' suggested an older man. 'Some people may need it more than others. Symbols help me, and fortunately my church isn't completely without them. But I don't think anyone there knows the difference between a sign and a symbol – or rather, how to be open to the symbolic.'

'If you think of it,' Joe suggested, 'each church generally caters for a limited range of human preferences and perceptions because of the choices it makes in environment and liturgy. Sure, there is music, but usually of a particular kind. There is intellectual interaction and there may be emotion, depending on the nature of the service. Some churches have incense and candles, which allows for more of the symbolic, while really contemporary churches display multiple TV screens that bring the platform activities to the back of the auditorium. Whatever the situation, there are a limited number of selected expressions and impressions to be gained from each church. That's quite understandable, but it may not allow for sufficient options to satisfy and help modern believers. The days of the minister and tradition deciding how worship is best conducted, on the basis that it should always be done in a particular way, are on the way out. A lot more creativity is needed, I would say; and a greater knowledge of what is available in our rich traditions would not go astray.'

'Are you saying that people leave the church because it's all too much of the same after a while?' someone commented.

'I think that can be an important factor,' Joe agreed. 'It could also be because they find it increasingly difficult to experience a faith that is alive, that is based on a personal relationship with Jesus Christ rather than on how the church conducts its business. Ministers may try to encourage such a relationship – some don't even do that – but that doesn't guarantee it will happen. Often what the church has on offer are religious practices, rather than a purposeful method that helps people become increasingly intimate with God. Receiving the right support from your church in facilitating personal growth may not be that easy. Unfortunately we haven't time in this lecture to take that subject further.'

'From a symbolic and artistic point of view,' continued Joe, 'we need briefly to consider icons and statues. During the Reformation in Protestant Europe more than four centuries ago, many churches were vandalised and much art was destroyed because it was considered to foster idolatrous practices. Of course there is that possibility: but should we stop drinking wine just because wine can make you drunk? I don't think so.' He paused, to allow for comments and questions. Joe liked to encourage interaction with his students, disliking the kind of lecture that is delivered to a politely silent audience.

'I don't need icons to connect with God. So why have them?' Somebody always came back with that point. A reasonable one, Joe thought.

'What exactly is an icon?' asked somebody else.

'A picture with spiritual significance, widely used in the Eastern Churches. Icons are very popular in the Russian and Greek Orthodox traditions. Historically, monks in particular have dedicated their whole lives to the painting of icons, many of which have become significant art

treasures. Icons can depict a biblical scene, or make a symbolic representation of truth and divine realities. Saints
too are often painted. Icons differ from mandelas, another
kind of spiritual art, in that the latter deal primarily with
the symbolic, not with people or narrative representa-
tions. In the twelfth century, for instance, Hildegard of
Bingen experienced many visions, which were painted as
colourful mandelas. She also dictated the meaning of each
picture. We will talk about Hildegard in another lecture,
but in the meantime you can find a book about her in the
college library.'

'Who has a photo at home of a significant family member
who is deceased?' Joe inquired. A few hands went up.
'Would it be wrong to look at the photo and remember
positive things about the person and take courage from
that? Of course it wouldn't! But what would happen if you
began to talk to the photo briefly because you felt that to be
helpful?'

Now the students began to disagree. Some thought it
would be acceptable, a harmless exercise. Others were not
so sure.

'It could lead to ancestor worship,' one student
objected.

'That's a bit far-fetched,' another responded.

'But it fits with the fact that if you venerate something
you could go on to adore it and eventually to worship it ...'

Joe intervened. 'Well – what if you were to ask the
person in the photo, who was a Christian and now dwells
in heaven, to intercede with God for you?'

Totally wrong, many of the students decided, though
not all.

'I relate to a particular Saint, and yes, I find it quite beneficial,' said one. 'But of course I don't *worship* him, it's just
a kind of identification,' she added.

'I appreciate that,' Joe said quickly. He could see a heated discussion could easily break out. 'Many Christians in the Catholic and Orthodox traditions are familiar with that practice, and receive benefit from it. Now there is indeed a big difference between seeking connectedness with a person who when alive was a great example of the Christian walk – and worshipping that person. Reflection on that person's life may well strengthen your own, and may perhaps open the door to the symbolic; but that doesn't make her or him divine. All divinity rests in God exclusively.'

'So you agree with the practice of icons?' one student challenged Joe.

'Perhaps I can best answer that by saying that in a large portion of the Christian church the practice is common,' he responded. 'Though I do not engage with it myself, I have decided not to pass judgment. After all it involves many people who will love God like I do. Christians have come to varying conclusions about icons and images. You'd do well to read the views held on both sides of the debate. There are some references in the course hand-out. I raised the matter because it's a good example of how intrinsic or extrinsic our spirituality is. By "extrinsic", I mean that you don't easily tolerate ideas different from your own; "intrinsic" means that you do. Healthy spiritual growth is considered intrinsic. It creates space for the other person and also for you. Imagine, if I were to ask you to walk around inside yourselves, how much space would you have? Think about it. Narrow-minded people tend also to be narrow-minded towards themselves. Often it's because they're insecure. Of course, being tolerant doesn't mean you have to agree with everything. There is much that I don't agree with, but I will try to understand and uphold people in their dignity regardless.'

Fair enough, Emma thought. But she wondered if Joe had lost sight of his original subject: art and spirituality. She need not have worried.

'It's all a matter of awareness of the other – the other person and the Other, called God. The better I know God, the greater the self-knowledge I will have and the more understanding I will have of others. There is a lovely story of the peasant of Ars in France centuries ago, who was known for his wisdom and piety. When he was asked how he prayed, he explained that he just looked at God and let God look back at him. Whoever looks at God is known by God; in response he or she will increase in self-knowledge. Awareness will grow, not just of God and self, but in a way that influences how you look at others and at everything else.'

'So, you need meditation?' a student suggested.

'Yes, or contemplation, or reflection, or spiritual reading – those prayer dynamics we have discussed before. The important thing, though, is that my development in awareness completely depends on how much I search for it. It's an attitude. How closed is my mind? How blind are my eyes? If ever I were to think, "I have no problems in that area," I'd be fooling myself. The way to see more clearly with my mind, my eyes, my intuition, my heart, my feelings, is to spend time with God.'

Emma decided to ask a question. 'You mean that I will get a clearer perception of the world around me?' The possibilities they were discussing were very much the basis of her approach to art; to see what wasn't usually seen that way, and somehow to make it known.

'Yes, exactly,' Joe agreed, welcoming the fact that Emma had joined in the discussion. 'As an art student, you're continually faced with this question of looking at things more intently and intuitively than is usual. But all of us have that ability, though we may not have the artistic talent to conceptualise it, in exceptional ways. Let me ask a slightly different question.' He looked around the group. 'Is there such a thing as Christian art?'

During the discussion that followed, various points of view were expressed. Emma sat and listened, until one of the students asked her how she would answer Joe's question. At this point in the discussion Emma had reached the conclusion that there was no such thing as Christian art: art was simply art. She said so. Joe listened, with a certain pleasure at her perceptiveness.

'OK,' he said, picking up the reins again. 'Here's another question. Is all art morally good?'

No, of course not, was the general consensus.

'Could someone who truly practises the Christian faith create a piece of art that was morally questionable?'

No, the students agreed. If they did, it would merely demonstrate that the artist's 'Christian spirituality' was a sham.

'So – isn't the question really a moral and possibly an ethical question, rather than a religious one?'

The students could see Joe's point.

'However, music, for instance – apart from the lyrics – isn't usually thought to fit into a moral category, because its nature is a spiritual nature. Thus besides the moral and ethical, the spirit of art is also important. An artistic expression can have a spirit that is unlike Christianity. The problem is, who decides? Is rap music acceptable in church, for instance? But I don't want to get into that now. The point is that art is art. There are standards that art has to meet if it is to be acceptable to Christians, and there is art that takes up Christian themes. But fundamentally, it's art; not "Christian art".'

The students nodded in agreement.

Time was up, and Joe needed to bring the discussion to an end. He had left his most important point until last.

'The real question for all of us is this: how able are we to look, to perceive, to hear and to create? Creativity is fundamental to all art. And we all have our own creative possibilities, but many people have their creativity locked up somewhere deep inside. Christian spirituality encourages creativity; and it starts with God. Get closer to God, and you will begin to see with both excitement and sadness. That's the essence of art. I started off by saying that art is everywhere, but that we don't see it. Art is also within us, and we are ignorant of it. I suggest you pray, and release that other part of you a little more.'

With that, Joe wished everyone a safe journey home. He thanked Emma for coming and chatted with a few students briefly. He was secretly pleased; Emma seemed to have enjoyed herself.

'So you agree with the practice of icons?' one student challenged Joe.

'It might be most helpful to answer that by posing a more fundamental question,' he responded. 'The question is, can God can deal with it? A large section of the church is familiar with the practice. If God can handle it, who am I to pass judgment? It seems to me that God is not speaking out clearly against it, otherwise many good Christians who use icons would have discovered God's displeasure with the idea. Considering that it concerns such a large portion of the church, God surely should be able to get a message of displeasure across somehow.'

11

Spiritual Friends

The dream had come back, and with a vengeance. Emma wasn't happy about it. She had actually forgotten about the dream, which wasn't difficult with so many other matters demanding attention. The funeral had been left at memory lane as well, somewhere in a shaded corner, and the downer she experienced soon afterwards was now history too. Joe's advice at the time had been helpful; she'd felt better after a few days of proper rest and relaxation. Herbal tea had helped her sleep like a log; one of the extra shifts at work had suddenly been cancelled; a minor break-through occurred with one of her art projects. Life had taken a turn towards normality. Except for the dream.

After her visit to Joe's home, Emma had resolved to try the spiritual exercises they had discussed. And she had done so, not as often perhaps as she initially intended, but regularly enough. The Jesus Prayer was a strange experience. At first, speaking audibly, she kept listening to herself and felt as if she were talking into the air. By persevering, and controlling her breathing, the feeling progressed from strange to almost comfortable. She had also begun to use the prayer mentally in different situations. It was hard to explain what the effects were, except to say that it was positive. At one point, when she was under pressure, to her surprise, she had turned to the prayer almost automatically and felt supported by it. Emma was fully aware that in using the Jesus Prayer she was calling on Jesus. It hardly could be any other way. But it was attractive, and seemed to affirm that Jesus had no difficulties at all with her using his name and that he didn't take it lightly either. Some might have thought that she was fooling herself. But Emma didn't think so.

The other exercise, reflective Bible reading, only worked successfully once. She tried it a few times, but on one particular occasion it had been really different. She was reading Psalm 23 in a relaxed and focused manner, when the words suddenly extended into another realm of awareness altogether and took on a life of their own. It was quite amazing. Soon she had stopped reading, for she could no longer concentrate. Then, lying on her bed, she dissolved into tears. A similar feeling had come over her some months ago. It was the feeling of being accepted and cared for – deeply spiritual, but very real. After a while, when things settled down, she found herself praying the Jesus Prayer. It wasn't long till she fell asleep on her bed.

All kinds of emotions had been touched upon in that experience, and she had needed a good cry. The next day she felt a different person, but over time that had begun to wear off. Now, a few weeks later, the wolf had suddenly returned; the same dream, but more frightening than before.

'I'm being followed by a wolf,' Emma said sheepishly to Joe. She had told him she needed a private talk, and he had invited her once again to his home. 'It's a dream, but it's more than a dream. The wolf seems to stalk me during the day.'

Joe pondered for a few moments in silence. Finally, he said, 'There is a way for Christians to help each other, called Spiritual Friendship. There's an older name for it, which I don't care for because it sounds too serious and authoritarian: Spiritual Direction. It's a very old practice. It is a way of listening together to God. I think it may help us. Would you like me to explain?'

'It sounds like therapy,' said Emma.

'Well, it may indeed be therapeutic, but I wouldn't call it therapy. It doesn't involve psychological analysis, nor does it try to solve any problems necessarily. What it aims to do is to discern what God might be saying about a given situation. In your case, what does the wolf mean?

'So how can a time of spiritual listening together with a friend help you discover what it means? It is not a talking process, although some discussion will happen; it's more a matter of reflecting together. It will therefore involve more silences than would be the case, for instance, in a counselling session.'

Emma gave it some thought. 'I don't think I'd be any good at listening to God,' she said.

Joe understood. 'Yes, that's fair comment. But you may surprise yourself. Anyway, I'd be happy just to talk about your dream, if you like.'

Emma seemed a little more comfortable now. 'I think I know what it means,' she confessed. 'But first I better tell you the whole dream.' She told Joe about the valley, the snow, the wolf and the need she had felt to get out over the hillside.

'So how do you interpret it?' Joe asked.

'Well, the wolf is a kind of shadow, a negative shadow.'

'Yes.'

'And the valley is my walk of life.'

That was a reasonable conclusion, Joe thought.

'The valley is deceptive, because it seems that things will be OK.'

'But they aren't?'

'No. The valley is probably not deadly – but I need to get out of it,' she explained, with conviction.

'So why don't you?' It was the key question.

'I don't know.'

Joe remained quiet, wondering what further explanations Emma might have for her dream. She just sat for a while, pondering the situation. On one level she knew very well why she had not yet escaped that valley. It had been clearly shown her some weeks ago, in the bus. Did she really want it enough, getting out? Yes, she did! But she wasn't doing it; or perhaps, she couldn't.

Joe asked, 'What's on the other side of the hill?'

Emma did not respond for a while. Then she replied: 'God'. Joe, she suspected, had probably figured that out already.

'And how do you feel about that?'

Her primary feeling at that moment was irritation; not with God, but with her reluctance to face up to the fact that she was being invited to bring faith back into her life. In fact, she wanted to do so, but somehow couldn't break into it.

'I feel confused and annoyed,' she admitted.

'Because of God?'

'No, because of me.'

Joe thought for a moment. 'I'm going to ask you a question', he said, 'which I don't want you to answer right away. Just reflect on it for a while. Is that OK?'

'Sure.'

'Consider this: Why would you turn away from love and acceptance?'

Emma looked briefly at Joe, then stared down at her hands, clasped in her lap. Why indeed would she turn away from love and acceptance? She couldn't answer the question. Suddenly she realised that this was central to how she felt. The easiest response would be to avoid the question, but that was no solution at all; it would show a lack of courage, and she simply did not want to be that sort of person.

'Listen, Emma,' Joe said kindly after a while, 'your problem may be one of honesty and integrity.'

'But I am an honest person.'

He smiled. 'Yes, indeed you are. Perhaps you feel that you can't honestly accept God's love, because though you feel just as significant as the next person, you still don't feel good enough for God.'

'You mean, I hold back because I need to feel acceptable enough by my own standards, before I can let God accept me?' Just saying it made Emma realise that this was part of her problem. But what could she do about it? Saying that it would be all right with God simply didn't do it for her. Her problem was beginning to take a much clearer shape.

'Perhaps you do place that qualification upon yourself. The point is, the day never comes when you will feel acceptable enough on the basis of your own merits. It's not unusual to want to feel like that, particularly with people who are honest about themselves, but it's the wrong approach.'

'What's the right approach?' asked Emma quietly.

'Ah,' Joe said, 'I can talk about that. But I'm not sure how effective it would be.'

'So?' Emma's question came out more sharply than she had intended.

'Sorry, Emma,' Joe apologised, 'I don't mean to be confusing. What I meant is that somehow you will need to see the whole truth about God's love. The penny needs to drop into your spirit, so to speak. Talking usually doesn't do that adequately.'

Emma was suddenly embarrassed, feeling that she had over-reacted to Joe's attempt to help her. 'I'm the one who should be sorry, Joe,' she said. 'It isn't your fault.' Her words poured out unbidden. 'I don't think I've ever thanked you for the help you are trying to give me.' That was as far as she managed to get. Then she began to choke on her words and had to stop.

'It's fine, Emma. Thanks for the appreciation. Don't worry about it,' Joe said. His voice betrayed emotion of his own. 'I'm going to make a pot of tea.'

With that he disappeared into the kitchen, leaving Emma to think matters over.

'Spiritual friends?'

'Spiritual friends,' Joe responded. He smiled broadly and raised his teacup in a mock toast. Emma returned his grin. They drank their tea in companionable silence. Emma was the first to break it.

'You want me to listen to God, don't you?' She had thought about their conversation while Joe made the tea.

'I think it might help.'

'I haven't told you about one of my spiritual reading times, the ones you encouraged me to do,' Emma continued. She told Joe the story of how God had brought Psalm 23 alive.

'You see, Emma,' Joe explained, 'God has shown you quite a few things and you have taken them in. But have you ever taken quality time to listen properly to what is being conveyed? I'm talking about reflective listening in your spirit, letting it sink in.'

Emma had to admit that she had not. Such a thing had never crossed her mind, and she had of course been largely unaware of the concept. 'So – I should listen?' she said, more to herself than to Joe.

Joe said nothing.

'OK, let's listen then.' Emma suddenly knew that this was what she would do. She could trust Joe, that was quite clear by now. And she'd better begin to trust God, for what was the point otherwise?

'We'll both listen,' Joe said. 'The idea is simple. There is a question that needs God's perspective. So we raise that question between ourselves and silently sit with it for a while before God together. If possible, we don't talk, not even much in our minds, but try to perceive what God's ideas are on the matter. The first question can be followed by another if necessary, but I doubt if that will be necessary today.'

'So we need a question. Have you got one?' Emma said.

'Well, yes. Though really it should be your question.'

'What's yours?'

'"What has God been trying to tell you?"'

'"What has God been trying to tell me?"' Emma repeated.

'Or Jesus, if you like. It makes no difference.'

'OK.'

'Don't think about the question, just sit with it and let it happen to you,' Joe said. 'I'll do the same. You can speak when you feel you want to.'

They sat together in silence for a while. Then Emma began to cry. She couldn't help it, and she didn't mind. Her tears flowed quietly.

Eventually she blew her nose. When she finally spoke, she didn't tell Joe all that she had felt. But she told him that she knew that God loved her, and that she could now walk out of that snow-covered valley. Joe didn't need to be told all Emma's discoveries. He had a good idea of what she would have been feeling, anyway.

He too had listened before God, but he never told Emma what he had perceived about her. He never told anyone, not even his wife Jane.

Joe had great difficulty in hiding his own tears. Being at heart an undemonstrative man who disliked drawing attention to himself, he mastered his emotion. He knew that Emma was going to be fine. There would be struggles, of course there would. But she would be fine.

It was a good feeling. In fact, it was a very good feeling.

12

The Prayer of Awareness

They were back at the coffee shop. After their last meeting they had planned to stay in touch, meeting every three or four weeks. It was enough. The last thing Joe wanted was to crowd Emma, who had told him of her determination to persevere with the spiritual side of life and obviously meant every word. Joe sipped his coffee with enjoyment. It was great to see her again.

'I've booked my trip to Europe.'

'And you're excited?' he asked.

'Very. Not long to go now! I've almost finished my studies. I can't wait to get on the plane.'

'That'll be excellent. Make sure you visit some cathedrals. If you go to Italy, perhaps you'll visit Assisi where St Francis came from. They say it's quite wonderful. But I'm sure you can plan your itinerary without my help!'

Emma smiled happily. 'I've already started visiting cathedrals.'

'You have?' Joe was a little surprised.

'Yes, for my studies, for an assignment. I have decided to use the cathedral here in town.'

Joe nodded, taking in the information.

'No more wolf,' said Emma.

'I'm glad.' Joe hadn't expected anything else. Still, it was good to hear. 'It won't bother you again.'

'No, it won't.'

Emma looked out across the familiar street. It wasn't hot this time of year. Spring was approaching, and the sun slanting in made all the colours look different. The early spring hues had their own attractiveness, though nothing like the bright colours of summer. It was true that softer light allowed for a greater variety of moods, but her own mood was more like summer. It had been so ever since their last meeting. Some personal issues had been resolved, it seemed, and she felt different.

'How is your art coming along?' Joe continued.

'Rather well, I think. But not as well as I would like.'

'Isn't that the artist's curse – never to achieve entirely what you feel is in you?'

'Yes, I suppose,' Emma admitted. She was familiar with the problem. 'It's a matter of how you look at things; whether you see adequately, and how to take it down. I appreciated what you said about human perception during your lecture.'

'Awareness', Joe reflected, 'is central to all of life, and not just the arts. Some people have called prayer that seeks intimacy with God a prayer of awareness, on the basis that getting closer to God makes you see things differently.'

'I remember you mentioning that.'

'Yes, real prayer makes you a better person. And a better artist.'

Emma stirred her cup for no real reason and said, 'Tell me some more about it.' Her desire for prayer had increased lately, and she found it easier.

'You mean about the prayer of awareness?'

'Yes: prayer and life, and art.'

'Sure,' Joe agreed.

*

'Prayer really is the best beginning you can make for anything. In essence it is a relational dynamic. It starts in the heart. The basis of all genuine Christian prayer is love. Prayer has been called the language of love.'

'I understand.' And Emma did understand; Joe had described her recent experiences with God. During that time of listening at Joe's home, God's love had been revealed to her in a special way. It was awesome and liberating. The same dynamic touches the world at large; she knew that now, even though the revelation had been a limited one. She sensed that love itself was huge, far beyond her capacity for understanding. But the experience had been sufficiently powerful to change her perception of things. It was difficult to explain. In future she would take her relationship with God, especially Jesus, seriously.

Joe looked at Emma. Her voice carried certainty, conveying that she really understood what he meant when he described love as the basis of all prayer. 'God always gives understanding', he said, 'to those who seek.'

'I feel I want to pray and read more. But it's usually difficult, and it's hard to find the time.'

'That's a normal reaction, and it can change. The problem is that many Christians never break through the initial stage of prayer. They tend to give up at that point, and find it hard to keep their faith alive. It all becomes too difficult, particularly when they sometimes find church more of a problem than a blessing – which can happen! You have to maintain your own faith; you can't expect others to do it for you. Of course it's possible to ride the crest of a wave when exciting things are going on at church or in your life. But what happens when the wave is past and the water is placid?' There was a note of urgency in his voice.

'Are you warning me, Joe?'

Joe smiled. 'I suppose I am, in a way. I'm just explaining life as I know it. I'd like to think that I'm actually
encouraging you, though it may not sound like that. A
relationship with Jesus has exciting prospects, and it is
never boring if you know how to maintain the connection.'

That's fair enough, thought Emma. She was a self-
reliant person, and if her faith was going to remain vibrant
she would rather take responsibility for it herself. In any
case, it didn't make sense any other way, for it was her
own relationship with God that mattered and not someone else's.

'When I say "prayer", it represents all our relational
activity with God,' Joe resumed. 'We've talked about that
before. I would include reflective reading of significant
books, not necessarily Christian, as long as our reading
allows for God to be present. Anyway, allow me to mention Teresa of Avila.'

'Another monk?' Emma said teasingly.

'A nun, this time,' Joe responded with a smile. 'She
lived in Spain in the sixteenth century, and was a friend of
John of the Cross.'

'The poet.'

'Yes, the poet.'

'You gave me a few lines of his poetry.'

'I remember. Well, Teresa was an incredible woman.
She identified four levels of prayer, which she compared
to four ways of watering a garden. The first is drawing
water by hand, for instance lowering a bucket into a well.
That's hard work, and you have to work very hard to get
small amounts of water. It's much like the beginnings of
prayer, when it's difficult and God doesn't seem to
respond very easily. A sense of closeness to God is hard to
come by, although there should be *some* perception of the

divine presence. But the whole exercise might not seem to be very worthwhile.'[1]

'Why should it be that hard? If God is love, why these difficulties? Could it not be easier?'

'A fair question,' Joe admitted. 'I think the problem might be that spiritual growth doesn't happen immediately. It takes time and perseverance. It's not that a beginner's prayer is void of blessings. There will be enough encouragement in it to keep pressing on towards a better awareness of God. But it shows that for prayer to become more natural to us, determination is essential. That's often where we fall short. Also, good prayer requires honesty before God, and many people prefer to avoid that difficulty.'

At one particular prayer time, which didn't feel like a particularly special time, Emma had been asked by God to own up to a small matter of which she became aware. So she could relate to Joe's point about honesty. Prayer could be like a mirror, she'd discovered, and what you saw about yourself wasn't always complimentary. There hadn't been any accusation, in her experience. It was more like an encouragement. But it showed her up all the same, and seemed to ask for an honest response.

'The second way of drawing water – the second stage of prayer – is easier,' Joe continued. 'Here, Teresa suggests it is like using a windlass – in modern terms, a pump. You get a better outcome for less labour. You feel that God is less difficult to find, and your prayers seem to be more meaningful. When you read the Scriptures, God appears really involved and better insights are revealed. Also

---

[1] St Teresa's method as Joe expounds it is based on the explanation given in Thomas H. Green, *When the Well Runs Dry: Prayer Beyond the Beginnings* (Ave Maria Press, 1980), 36–55.

you'll experience more integration as a person in your soul. At this second stage, you will notice that an awareness of God remains with you, more continually, every day.'

'Is that the prayer of awareness you were talking about?'

'Yes, it is.'

'I'm not that spiritual. I'm certainly not a nun. But do you think that I could do that?' she suggested.

'You could,' said Joe. 'Quite well actually, if you practised the kind of things we have been talking about during our meetings.' He was encouraged by the amount of interest that Emma was showing.

'OK,' she said, raking her right hand through her hair like a comb. She sounded convinced.

'Well, you'll need God's help of course, but that is always available. Eventually, when you have advanced somewhat in this second stage, you should experience what Teresa called the prayer of quiet, which we have talked about before.' He paused.

'Would you like another coffee? Maybe a juice?' Emma offered. She felt like a short break, and was enjoying sitting in the sun in a friendly crowded environment.

'I'd love another coffee,' said Joe.

'In essence, the prayer of quiet is contemplative prayer. That means, it seeks stillness and avoids activity. It is a prayer of love, coming from the heart rather than the mind. Thoughts and imagination try not to interfere with the heart's intuition and perception of the divine presence. The praying person is drawn into this presence without personal effort, apart from just being available and handing over personal control mechanisms. The dynamic is initiated and carried by God in response to you selecting quietness as the basis for prayer. When you become familiar with the experience, you can enter in quite easily. Afterwards you might question whether you really were praying at all, for it took no effort.'

'So I start to meditate.'

'Sort of. You may remember that meditation has more of a personal emphasis, like imagination or reflection about an idea, text or object. By all means start with that, but the purpose of the prayer of quiet is to leave your meditation behind and just be with God, while avoiding mental activity as much as possible. It is called "apophatic" prayer, which means "without words and images". This technique goes way back, to well before the time of Christ.'

'It sounds like Buddhism.'

'Yes, Buddhism is apophatic,' Joe agreed. 'Of course, we are not seeking nirvana, but God's presence. That is a totally different focus. In Christianity, this prayer approach simply means that you are willing not to let your limited human abilities of thought and speech restrict your possible perceptions of God. There is a famous Christian book called *The Cloud of Unknowing*, written in the Middle Ages in England by an unknown author. It presents the Christian tradition of apophatic prayer. You'll probably come across it one day. It instructs us to put a *cloud of forgetting* beneath us (which means leaving all earthly thought and memories behind), and to reach out into the *cloud of unknowing* above us. "Unknowing" refers to the fact that normal thought processes are very limited in discovering who God is. The only language that can enter the cloud is the language of love, a language of the heart. So, open your heart and close your head, so to speak, as much as possible. You may then begin to receive, as a divine gift, what normally cannot be humanly understood. It's rather mystical, in a sense, but not impossible for a sincere praying person to become familiar with this type of prayer. Everybody has got a measure of mystical ability anyway, if only it were developed.'

'I can be mystical?' That didn't sound too bad, thought Emma.

'Yes, contemplative prayer is a kind of mystical prayer, though I wouldn't call it mysticism. Anyway, that would lead me too far away from our topic,' Joe decided. 'For people like us', he concluded, 'a contemplative experience of less intensity is more within reach.'

'What are Teresa's other two stages?' asked Emma.

'Well, those are rather mystical, and happen entirely at God's instigation. The third stage is the garden watered by a stream or a brook. In this experience, prayer really saturates your soul. It's more of God and less of you. And the fourth stage, where the garden is watered by heavy rain, takes it a step further still, and brings you into the presence of God in a way that makes you feel you are completely absorbed into the divine presence – without, however, losing your identity. In fact, you are finding your true identity. But as this identity is fully in God, without earthly psychological baggage, there seems to be little differentiation between you and God. The experience is usually referred to as "divine union". But again, that needs much more discussion. Mind you, these last two stages of prayer, which Teresa presents from her own experience, are not something that you and I are likely to find happening to us.'

Joe quickly glanced at his watch. 'There's one more important aspect of the prayer of awareness that I'd like to highlight, if that's OK?'

Emma nodded and sat quite still. Her mind had been working overtime.

'The prayer of awareness has been called that because it makes you more aware of how God might look at the world, and at you personally. You can carry that awareness along with you wherever you go, and it can grow and become sharper. It is a kind of awakening. It is, in fact, the result of a contemplative approach to life that is anchored in the prayer methods we have discussed. The insights from your prayer times will be deposited permanently, though obscurely, in your conscious and your subconscious. You will receive God-given insights quite apart from prayer in the normal daily activities of life. This kind of living involves your whole being, which at every moment desires to be in contact with the Source of all life, who is the great I AM. It is a mode of being alive that derives from the being of God as much as possible. You carry the resulting awareness into everything you are and everything you do. It is the beginning of a contemplative life, and it has wonderful possibilities.'

The discussion had reached a natural stopping point. Emma tried to absorb all she had learned. She understood, or could at least appreciate the value of, what Joe had just explained. Joe, for his part, hoped he hadn't made the explanation too dense and compact. 'I'll e-mail you some readings on what we've been talking about,' he promised.

'You're saying that if I develop a prayer life that includes the prayer of quiet, I can live as you have just described?' asked Emma.

'With God's help – yes, you can. But it is not an easy road. John the Baptist said about Jesus, "He must increase and I must decrease." Still, it is the road to freedom. Jesus told us that he came to set us free. Not by us agreeing with him that it is a great idea, but by him really working it out with us in our lives and liberating us. We also need particularly to be liberated from ourselves.'

Emma didn't know what to say. It seemed that Joe had just mapped out her life before her. Was that what she wanted? Undoubtedly, that powerful experience of Jesus' love some weeks ago was behind it all. She felt a strong invitation and a wonderful promise, for her art as well as herself.

'To be or not to be?' she concluded.

'Yes,' Joe agreed. 'That's the question.'

'You look tired,' she told him.

He smiled. 'I'm fine,' he reassured her. He would miss Emma, he told himself, when she left for Europe.

Sacred Spaces and Detachment

Emma had decided to sit in the cathedral to do some reflecting. She liked the environment; it was a sacred place. It created a sort of distance between her and the world outside – the sort of space she needed right now. The building was beautiful and spacious, did not press in upon her, and projected a sense of permanency and history. It had a presence that was attractive to Emma and she enjoyed the artistic eloquence of its architecture and furnishings.

But more importantly, it invited her to come to rest. Emma sat quite still and allowed the cathedral to address her soul. She could hear people moving around at the front of the building, but it wasn't intrusive. After a while her thought patterns began to settle down and entered into a kind of drifting, as she called it. By now she had enough experience of reflective prayer for this to happen. Drifting with God ... her eyes, though not closed, had lost their focus. Eventually she did close them and briefly began to say the Jesus Prayer in her spirit.

The decision to visit the cathedral had been prompted by the difficulty Emma had experienced in finding the kind of space in her life that she needed, to address some significant questions properly. Some of the readings that Joe had sent her had started the ball rolling. They

highlighted issues with which Emma was vaguely familiar, and which she now felt should be resolved; or at least,
she should get a handle on them. Her attention had been
particularly drawn to some pages on the teachings of
Meister Eckhart and the concept of 'detachment' – which
promised a freedom of spirit that was very appealing.

She had re-read those pages several times until she was
familiar with their contents, and had prayed about the
matter. But she needed to sit with the idea reflectively, to
give it some quality spiritual time; and so she had come to
the cathedral.

'Your main motivation in life, Emma,' someone once
told her, 'is success.' She'd been taken aback; but thinking
about it, she realised that the comment had been perceptive. She couldn't deny that success was important to her.
It gave her the prestige and security she craved. She hated
failure in herself, and could barely tolerate it in others. She
would rather mix with those who seemed to have got it
together. Occasionally, in the past, she had noticed that she
would not baulk at telling a white lie, if it protected her
identity as a person of some capability.

Luckily for a potential artist, she had enough talent to
be amongst the top students in her year. She didn't like to
think how she'd feel if that were not so. In her defence
(and Emma had a number of ways of justifying herself),
she worked hard for her achievements. Success, however,
is a demanding taskmaster, and totally untrustworthy as a
basis on which to build your life. Emma had sensed that
for some time now, but had never felt able to address the
problem adequately.

Of course, setting goals was fine. Getting things done
was OK. And there was no reason at all why being an
achiever shouldn't be enjoyable and have its rewards. But
was the desire for success dictating to her? Or did she see it
as something worthwhile but finally not indispensable?

She suspected that the desire for success had taken more of a hold than she would have wished; and it was a pressure she could do without. Success was a debilitating driving force if you were its slave, rather than the invigorating energy she felt it should be. And then she had read about detachment.

It seemed that the word 'salvation', as used by the church to describe the mission of Jesus Christ, originally meant 'being led into a large place', or 'giving you plenty of space'. It has to do with living, without oppression, a life without deceitful taskmasters. An internal life, one that allows the freedom to be yourself, rather than trying to be the person you invent in order to cope with matters of identity and significance.

While still quite young, Emma had noticed that being successful brought considerable praise from others. It made her try even harder. She began to tell herself that she needed success, and she became impatient with people whose priorities were different. In fact, her rapid assessments of others did not allow them much space at all. She understood now: she should be more tolerant. The whole situation was less than admirable. It needed changing. A picture of her mother suddenly came into her mind, and the first pangs of remorse set in.

To find space, you need to give space, Emma had discovered. Joe said something similar when he asked the students at his lecture how much space they had to walk around within themselves. How much space do I have? Emma thought. Part of that space was taken by the dual oppressors, success and the fear of failure. Another area was occupied by her tendency to be opinionated. Then there was her unwillingness to forgive those who had created negative experiences, the hurts and loneliness, while she was growing up. She conveniently forgot all the good things that had happened during that time. Or rather, she didn't forget them but refused to allow them to offset the bad memories.

So much stuff crowding my internal space, Emma thought. It was becoming clear that she needed to deal with it. Her freedom as a person depended on doing so. With some of it she might well be facing a lasting battle, but at least she now understood the dynamics involved.

Detachment is an attitude, she had discovered. You can train yourself in it. It doesn't mean being disinterested in others or in the surrounding world, but creating some space internally between the external and yourself. It was similar to solitude. Detachment needed a measure of self-control to stop you getting drawn in emotionally, or even just getting involved, where that would be unwise. It means taking a step aside even from your own opinions, or at least holding those lightly. She had learned that taking yourself too seriously should be avoided, and that she should not presume to understand easily how others are feeling or how they ought to act.

Don't even always insist on understanding your own feelings; don't become subject to your presumed reputation and status; don't become preoccupied with owning things. That might be difficult if you sold a painting you liked, one that revealed your soul, Emma thought. It should be just a painting, or rather, no more than a painting. Would she be detached enough to let it go, even though she loved the piece? From it, others might discover things about her, her moods and deeper emotions, which she would have rather kept to herself. Perhaps that would be a challenge one day.

Meister Eckhart even encouraged you to leave your ideas about God behind, in the knowledge that those ideas could merely be your own projection of what you thought God should be like. That would limit your ability to discover the divine nature more fully. It was all a matter of letting go, even of your entrenched ideas about God, and in that way restoring everything in its essential freedom. Then you could enjoy life, or if you suffered, would do so in existential integrity and wholeness – a position by nature both spiritual and relational, and best achieved with God's help.

Emma was convinced that without applying her faith and using prayer, she didn't have much chance of succeeding. And without taking it seriously, it wasn't even worth trying. So it came about that Emma sat in the cathedral, aware of the need to have the principles of detachment and forgiveness properly anchored in her spirit. She wanted to be as free as she could be – not selfishly so, but truly free. Emma knew that she should set others free also, particularly her mother.

It's a matter of sacred space, Emma concluded. Sacred space inside you, in which your spirit may roam free. She understood that a contemplative approach to life might achieve this, and that the idea of seeing yourself and the world around you more clearly was also connected with it. That process of finding sufficient space could be facilitated by external spaces like this cathedral, or the countryside, of course. Growing up in a rural area had taught her to appreciate the healing powers of a vast land that reflected eternal qualities. She remembered that in those days she had a favourite spot where she went to sort things out, halfway up a hill, with a view that stretched for miles across open spaces. Emma didn't mind the city, but in her spirit she remained a person of the land. She couldn't imagine ever losing that sense of belonging to places where horizons lead into deserts.

Her reflective time in the back of the huge church was restful, and also sensitive. Without looking, she could feel the vast space in which she was situated, a space that was comforting rather than threatening. It did not dictate her feelings, as some spaces might do, and it seemed to invite her to enter into her own inner space. The realisation came intuitively; it had a sacred quality; it was like a homecoming, she concluded, a sensation that originated in her heart.

Emma felt encouraged. While she was sitting there with God, neither the issue of detachment nor of forgiveness entered her intuitive processes. She wasn't problem-solving in this prayer time and hadn't intended to do so. She simply had come to sit in God's presence, convinced that this was necessary at that time for her spiritual well-being. Just being, with God, in space, is what she needed. She sensed, however, that the essential qualities of detachment and forgiveness, and the need to practise them, were becoming firmly planted in her spirit, as she hoped they might be. The two principles seemed to reach beyond the cognitive stages and were beginning to settle into a deeper part of her being. It was rather obscure, but real enough.

She felt that she was still free to ignore those principles in her life. That was always so, but it was exactly the kind of freedom from which she was trying to escape. She needed the freedom of sacred spaces, not the pseudo-freedom that told you to do as you please. That kind of freedom was just bondage in disguise – bondage to self, and all the baggage which that brings.

The busyness in the cathedral had increased. More people were moving about. Emma decided that her time was up. The organ sounded a few tentative notes, a pre-liminary test by the organist, who must have been satisfied that all was well; soon the cathedral was filled with the most beautiful music. It rolled like a wave between the high walls and into the apex of the roof, before bouncing back and falling upon the listeners below.

Emma sat entranced, allowing the music to carry her. Her surroundings, filled with symbolic meaning, seemed to reach another level of reality. It was quite amazing and inexplicable. Momentarily the experience lifted her soul into awe and wonder, and then began to drift away.

'The angels have been passing by and have moved on,' decided Emma, and wondered where that notion had come from. She stood up slowly. As she walked out, the organ music, growing ever fainter, followed her into the street, the sunshine and the traffic.

14

Discernment and Dark Nights

It was six or seven weeks since Joe and Emma had last met. Now they were sitting at an outside table at the coffee shop. It was well into spring and the sun was shining brightly; the street was full of shoppers, the air full of energy. Emma was enjoying the invigorating sensation of heat in her bones. Joe was just pleased to see her again and to see that she seemed happy.

They chatted for a while before Emma told Joe about her experience in the cathedral.

'It's very worthwhile and necessary to find that space you're talking about,' Joe observed. 'Maybe you should go on a retreat one day.'

'You mean, go somewhere special?'

'Yes, to spend time with God for a few days. It can be quite an experience. You can do it all by yourself, of course, but it is also helpful to join a structured retreat, under the supervision of a spiritual director or guide.'

'OK,' Emma said. It was an idea to keep in mind for later.

'Ignatius Loyola, the man who founded the Jesuits in the sixteenth century, was a great believer in retreats. For the members of his Order, he designed a retreat that takes a month to complete.'

'A whole month! That's a long time.'

'It is, but Ignatius didn't believe that really hearing from God was an easy matter. "There are so many voices interfering with the voice of God," he would say, "and it takes time to discern the movements in our spirits." The retreats were held, as they still are today, in accordance with his instructions. They are known as the "Spiritual Exercises". Some retreat masters have condensed them into as little as eight days; others use only part of them. Of course, many retreats don't use Ignatius at all.'

'If it is so difficult to hear from God, how can a normal Christian ever do it?' Emma asked.

'That's a good question,' Joe admitted. 'I don't want to give the wrong idea here. Hearing God doesn't have to be difficult; in fact you can follow God's voice each day without even being aware of it. Don't forget that the spirit of God dwells in you, not as some addition to your own spirit, but as completely you. It's a mystery, but true. Your conscience, your mind, your feelings and emotions are all continually influenced by God. Common sense, for instance, is a wonderful God-given quality. Our natural faculties are very much involved in our perceptions and activities for God. So God is near and effective in helping us in our lives. It's when people say, "The Lord specifically told me something", that caution is needed. Our own psychology can tell us many things that can be wrongly construed as God's voice. That's why special care is needed in this area of spiritual perceptions.'

'But there would be times when you really do hear from God in a special way,' Emma suggested. She had had some experience of that by now.

'That's very true,' Joe agreed. 'And there are times when knowing the mind of God would be really helpful. Let's think about that.'

*

'The Bible mentions certain spiritual gifts that are available to the church, such as wisdom, knowledge, and faith. They can be used prophetically in particular situations, and that's valid; believers in that case are articulating what they feel God seems to be saying in the situation. However, it is always necessary to evaluate the accuracy of a particular revelation or insight. It's sensible to discuss whatever is perceived as coming from God, with those who are experienced in discernment.'

Emma remembered hearing about spiritual gifts years ago at church.

'There is also, of course, significant value in seeking the mind of God on your own by spending time in prayer – just God and you privately,' Joe added.

'Fair enough,' said Emma. 'But how can one safeguard quality discernment, if there are such pitfalls?'

'You can keep a number of key factors in mind,' suggested Joe. 'First – and this might seem rather negative – don't expect crystal-clear answers very often. Discernment may come gradually and possibly only partially. God generally doesn't write letters from heaven. But you'll find out enough to make a significant response possible.

'Second, you have to analyse carefully the dynamics involved in how you receive your insight. Discernment very much involves sensing, intuition and thought. It is set against the background of how you are feeling at that moment. So you need to be careful in your perceptions. The help of a good spiritual guide can be very beneficial.'

'But if I don't have a spiritual guide', said Emma, 'where does that leave me?'

Joe smiled broadly. 'In the same boat as me! But all isn't lost. There are some helpful pointers we can keep in mind. For a start, I must be sure that I really want to hear from God, and I must make sure I don't bring my own agenda to the encounter. It can happen. The best safeguard is a desire for humility and honesty. That will prevent many mistakes.

'One of the greatest pitfalls is pride. For instance, what is the outcome of my discernment? Will it elevate me personally, in my importance and wealth – or will it be merciful, beneficial to others and to creation? The former can involve pride, while the latter is a clear expression of the nature of God. Ignatius referred to these dynamics as the good and evil movements in our spirits. There are many voices in our spirits and there are many dynamics in our circumstances. The best discerning is done not on the mountaintops or in the valleys, but on level ground. Never make a major decision when you are too elated or too depressed; it's a recipe for disaster. Also, you need to be patient and unhurried. It can take time to discern correctly what God's idea is on a certain matter.

'And finally, don't seek discernment if you are not willing to follow through on what it shows you. The outcomes of discernment are to help you towards life and love and truth and freedom.'

Joe, who considered discernment to be a key to maintaining a vibrant spiritual life, had spoken with conviction. There is always much in life that can take your joy away, he reflected; the spiritual life could easily drift into complacency. It is essential to keep in touch with God and with the movement of God's Spirit.

'There's an awful lot to remember,' said Emma. 'Can you summarise it in an e-mail for me later?'

'I'll remember to do that,' Joe promised.

He stretched in his chair. It was a beautiful day. 'Would you like a juice?' he asked. That was all there was to do here: drink and talk. It suited him fine. The better moments in life often came from engagements like this, and as friends mutually searching for the spiritual life they were relaxed in each other's company by now. 'I'll get it,' insisted Emma, and Joe suppressed his usual instinct to want to pay.

They sat in companionable silence for a few minutes, sipping their drinks and watching pedestrians passing by. Emma was the first to break the silence.

'What's the dark night of the soul?'

'How did you come across that?'

'It was in a book I read. It sounded important.'

'It is,' Joe said. 'And if you keep on growing spiritually, it could happen to you one day.'

'It sounds a bit scary.'

'It can be, according to John of the Cross. But not for us lesser mortals. The scary bit is reserved for the real mystics who follow the apophatic path in a big way. It can be intimidating to be scrutinised by a God who is a holy fire.'

'But it could happen to me?'

'Yes, it could. The dark night experience comes to many Christians. It is a real experience, though it is often not recognised for what it is.'

'So how will I recognise it?'

'In various ways,' he explained. 'It's a process of growing closer to God that is based on the "more of God, less of me" principle. The "less of me" is central to the dark night, and deals with the part of you that holds you back from achieving greater psycho-spiritual health. It includes a reduction of those influences that come from unhealed areas deep in your psyche. God works towards wholeness and wants to release you from unhealthy attachments – both the ones you know about and also the ones you don't. The dark night is essentially a stripping process towards greater health and freedom. It always originates with God.'

'More detachment,' Emma noted perceptively.

'Yes, that's right – progressively so. Before you enter a spiritual experience that might be classified as a dark night, you will usually feel a kind of dryness coming into your spirit for some time beforehand. It's so that you will let more go, so that you won't be so busy with your own activities – even with prayer. You will simply want to sit with God and say nothing, which is a desire too few Christians are familiar with. You may also start to question your attachments in life, both material and personal, such as your need for status and a good reputation.

'Unless you realise that this kind of spiritual activity is beneficial rather than destructive, you may interpret the flatness of your spirit as a sign that you are losing your faith, for your contact with God may seem unreasonably dull. It's quite possible for a person to stop the spiritual movement at the onset of a dark night if the experience is misunderstood. You can wrestle yourself out of it (though that is hard work) by using your willpower and faith. God will honour that, and stop the process, if you really insist.'

Emma listened intently. The dark night might come upon her one day, and she had no intention of missing the point if it did.

Joe continued. 'Of course there are other reasons for dullness of spirit, and you'll need to check that out – sinfulness, perhaps; illness or exhaustion; or a lack of prayer and spiritual reading. But if those parts of your spiritual life are in good shape and your spirit still begins to lose its usual sharpness, then probably you are being invited into spiritual desert country.'

'I don't mind deserts,' Emma said. 'In fact I quite like them. It's so pure and unspoiled and uncontrollable. The desert is fascinating.'

'Then you'll understand what I am going to say. Deserts play a major role in Scripture, as you may have discovered. And there is a beautiful quality in spiritual dryness, if you can only see it. One outcome of the dark night might be a better appreciation of the detached contemplative side of spirituality. According to St John, it is best not to go back to wordiness in prayer, but to increase your ability to just be with God intuitively and in silence.

'Anyway, let's concentrate on the actual experience. In the dark night, you feel that the heavens are like brass. You seem to lose your faith, and become very heavy in spirit. In fact you have just enough energy for your job and your duties at home, but beyond that you just want to sit and feel depressed. You can't pray, it doesn't work; and you can't read, for your mind does not register. But it is a strange kind of depression. God seems miles away and yet near, but you can't make a connection. Your heart longs for the spiritual – the last thing you want to do is turn your back on it – but it's dryness everywhere. You've entered the dark night.'

'Dry like a desert,' Emma suggested. 'But is there beauty in it? In the desert you feel very small and powerless, and everything is dry, but it is full of splendour.'

'Yes, it can have a beauty all of its own, if you are able to see it. The first rule is not to worry about the dark night and not to fight it. Just ride the wave for as long as it lasts. In God's timing, it will suddenly stop and you will feel much better than when it started. A permanent change for the better will have been achieved.'

'So what happens?'

'It's a purification and healing process. All of us need to be liberated from the baggage that we have gathered since childhood and still carry with us. Some of that baggage is so threatening that consciously, we can't handle facing it. Therefore, always be careful about stirring up deeply submerged issues, unless God initiates it. During the dark night, God deals with a lot of that baggage without ever showing you exactly what is being addressed. That Godly activity, deep within you, affects the conscious part of your spirit. It takes away your energy, probably so that the deep work can take place without major interruptions; and that's why you feel so very flat. Then is not the time to be spiritually active, and God will prevent it, until the healing work has been completed. So you just endure, relax and – if you can – actually enjoy it a little.' Joe fell silent.

'Well, I asked for that,' Emma said. 'It sounds quite an experience.'

Joe smiled. 'Don't worry, Emma. The dark night comes without you asking for it, perhaps only once or twice in your life, for a few days or a few weeks. Only God knows. But you'll always be fine, and much the better for it.'

15

Scoring Goals

In the distance, a twenty-foot boat was rocking slightly as two youths hoisted the mainsail. It was a good day for sailing; a steady breeze and a fairly flat sea. Joe and Emma were watching the goings-on at the marina from a nicely situated restaurant table with a view over the moored boats and the waters beyond. It was warm and pleasant, a promise of a hot summer to come. Joe loved the sea. He was imagining what it would be like to sail out, over the horizon. Emma was thinking about a similar release from moorings, but for her it would mean soon boarding a plane for Europe.

Emma had invited Joe for lunch as a thank-you. It would be their last meeting together. 'The French say that departing is a bit like dying,' said Joe. He was feeling a mixture of sadness and encouragement. He'd come to appreciate Emma for her perceptiveness, courage and integrity. Though he didn't know where her art would take her, he was sure she was going to do well. He admired creativity, and wished that more people would take the time to develop that side of their personality. In his own way he had been reasonably creative all his life. He looked out across the marina. Maybe he should think about buying a proper boat? He was getting too old to mess about in dinghies. But would he have time to enjoy it? There was so much to do, so many interest avenues waiting to be explored. Maybe one day.

Emma looked at Joe's familiar, kindly face. Even now, she didn't know very much about him. He wasn't secretive, but it had happened that almost all their conversations had been about spiritual matters. She suspected that Joe had been happy to leave it that way, not wanting to complicate their friendship with his own history.

And yet, she realised, she had in fact come to know him quite well. He had sometimes talked about his background, but more importantly he had been quite transparent about his faith, which was central to everything he did and everything he was. One thing she knew for certain, Joe had no illusions about his own shortcomings as a spiritual instructor. It had been a journey for both of them, for Joe seemed always to be searching. It was the main reason she felt she could trust him. Over the years Joe seemed to have kept his faith. 'Because God helped me keep it,' he would say, but Emma was sure it wasn't quite that simple. Or, perhaps it was; and it was that very simplicity that eluded people, who saw their faith lose its vibrancy or disappear altogether. Which prompted a question:

'What's a simple way to keep your faith alive?'

'Good heavens,' Joe laughed, 'how many simple answers do you want?' It was a typical Emma question: intuitive and going straight for the jugular. But it was a great question.

'Never give up on the last goal.'

'Sorry?'

'You're a soccer player, so you know that some matches are won in the last minute.'

Emma nodded. She could remember matches where that had happened.

'It's the same with faith. You have to keep trying to score that next goal, even if the opposition is powerful.

There's always a lot of resistance. The good thing is, the final whistle never blows, not even when we die. There's always time for another goal, because the game goes on. And anybody who seriously gives it a try will be a winner.'

'How simple is that!' There was a touch of sarcasm in Emma's voice.

'I know,' Joe said. 'But it's actually true. Of course, the real question is, "How can you continue playing the game without running on empty?" Expectations have a lot to do with it.'

A waitress arrived at their table with the salads they had ordered. Joe took a sip of his beer. Two light beers, two salads, he thought to himself. From the extensive menu they had both made the same choice.

There was a period of sustained munching. The salad was superb. Joe returned to the discussion.

'Imagine you're playing a team which is well below you in the League, and you're expected to win. Games like that can be dangerous, because the other team might be stronger than you expected. And life can be like that, too.' He reached for the salad dressing.

'You mean you can be mentally under-prepared?'

'Quite so. Perhaps because you told yourself that you'd win easily, or someone might have told you that you would. And in the same way you can sometimes get the impression with Christianity that the game has already been won by Jesus and all you have to do is to take the field.'

'And that's not true?'

'Well – the game has been won, of course it has. The final outcome is a given. But there is still an opposition on the field, and you're still required to kick your goals. As a player, you can get hurt; you will have to get up, take courage, work hard and get the job done. It is a task that needs conditioning. Nobody should play a game without training for it. And that's also part of the deal.'

'So there is no lazy way.'

'No. But you are bound to succeed if you keep an eye on the coach and aren't too perturbed when your fellow-players let you down. That can happen. Or it might be you who disappoint others. It's never easy. Join the club! It's all part of the game.'

He smiled ruefully. 'The club, by the way, is known as the church. Quite a club! The church is facing real challenges in maintaining its relevance to the modern world. I'm certain that it will adapt, and that under God's guidance it will succeed. But you shouldn't take anything for granted.'

'The newspapers are always pointing out the church's shortcomings,' Emma said. 'Actually, that throws me, a little. Churches seem to have often lost their way these days.'

'Yes, it is sad,' Joe agreed. 'So make sure you have your own personal strength. You can't survive on a second-hand faith; don't blame your fellow players when things don't work out; consult the coach. It's when the players lose contact with the coach that the big trouble starts.'

'I've joined the club, I think. But I haven't got a team yet.' She had wondered about this, but it wasn't yet a major problem. She would be travelling soon and had no idea where she would settle after that.

'But that doesn't have to stop you scoring some goals,' Joe replied. 'It is essential that you do.'

'Is everything OK?' asked the waitress.

'It's lovely,' said Emma. 'Can we have two more beers?'

As she went to get them, Joe busied himself with the last of his salad. It was a wonderful day. Great for relaxation, and for having a good time.

'You know, there are a few goals you can kick while you're travelling. Quite a few, in fact. I expect you know what they are, from our conversations together.'

Yes, there were plenty, Emma thought gratefully. She had created a small routine for herself, facilitating a relationship with Jesus. It was working reasonably well and was a great help. It was a start.

'One thing I haven't mentioned yet, which might be a good idea, is that you might like to keep a reflective journal.'

'I used to keep a diary when I was a teenager,' said Emma.

'And you probably stopped because life took over?' Joe suggested.

'Yes.'

'Try to keep one, and make sure you take the time to do it properly. Just record your thoughts, feelings and your experiences in light of your faith. You might be amazed how helpful that can be. You could also draw some mandelas and write out what they mean to you. Also, pray through the content of your journal reflectively.'

Emma agreed that it seemed a good idea. She promised to try it out.

'Do you like reading?' Joe asked, 'I mean, for relaxation?'

Emma did.

'Always have two books at hand apart from the Bible. One for pleasure, one for spiritual food.'

'OK!' That didn't sound too difficult.

'Another goal,' said Joe. 'Wherever you are, go and sit regularly for a while in a church. You may even wish to attend a service or two. You may be blessed, or educated, or both.'

Emma agreed to this as well.

'And two more,' Joe continued. 'Make sure that you share with others: your possessions, your talents, your forgiveness – whatever is merciful and needed. It will stop the flow of your faith from blocking up.'

'And the last?' Emma asked with some curiosity.

'Listen to people. Try, as often as you can, to really listen to people. Hear their stories. It's the best spiritual education you could wish for.' That's where most significant changes in life originate from, he reflected, but he didn't say it aloud. Emma would find it out for herself.

It was an unexpected final admonition, but she knew intuitively that Joe was right. I'll miss him, she thought. As he returned her gaze, Joe's heart dropped a little. He wished he could will that fine young person sitting across from him to succeed. But it wasn't his call. He would pray instead.

Emma stood up and went to pay the bill. This, their last meeting, was nearly over. In a few days' time she would be flying off. First, she was going home to say goodbye to her mother. She was actually looking forward to that, and knew that she had a job to do there before she left.

She came back to the table. Joe was standing, a book in his hand. He handed it to her. She recognised the author.

'The first dead monk you ever told me about,' she smiled.

'Just a little gift,' said Joe.

'It's wonderful, Joe.' She gave him a spontaneous peck on the cheek. 'Would you mind walking me to my car?'

Joe was more than happy to. They arrived at Emma's well-travelled small blue car. She opened the boot and carefully lifted out a framed painting. 'What do you reckon?' she asked. She was proud of this particular piece of work, and planned to develop its concept and style further.

He recognised the scene immediately. It was the wall in the shopping arcade, with the window that reminded him of the Shakers. Emma had painted it with just two people standing in front of it talking. Somehow the painting projected a sense of simplicity, space and hope. In some ways it was even reminiscent of the desert, perhaps because Emma had used different colours to those of the wall.

'It's beautiful,' he said. Then, 'Unbelievable,' he added, for this painting really spoke to him.

'I got a prize for it,' Emma explained.

'No wonder.' Joe was still looking at the painting as Emma held it up. 'Thanks for showing me, Emma.'

For a moment Emma didn't trust her voice. Then she said, 'It's yours, Joe.'

Joe now looked into her face and tears began to well up in his eyes, but he held them back. Emma held the painting out to him and slowly Joe took possession of it.

'Thanks for everything,' she said. 'I'll stay in touch.'

With that Emma turned, got into her car, and drove, with a slightly smoking exhaust pipe, out of Joe's life and into her future.

Emma's Little Notebook

Ideal for on the road

1. • Being before doing!

2. • To your real self be true
   • Be careful with self-talk
   • Spend quality time with yourself
   • Jesus is <u>always</u> involved
   • Only with Jesus can I become really myself

3. ———

4. • Meaning comes through revelation and is relational. It is given by the other.
   • Self-understanding comes to me in private
   • Only intimacy with Jesus will sufficiently actualise my true self.
   • Loneliness describes the pain of being alone, solitude the glory of being alone. (Paul Tillich)
   • Solitude allows me to carry a space between me and wherever I am. Fewer dictates from the outside – more my real self.

5. • Worship = adoration, communication, request
   • Intercession = persistent prayer on behalf of others and situations
   • Prayer Warfare = speaking into being by faith against spiritual opposition.

- Meditation = seeking enlightenment through a purposeful and reflective focus on an object, communication or imagination.
- Contemplation = a calm dwelling upon God without word, thought or image.

6. • Be a place-maker
   - Places of real belonging are given by others
   - Silence means to stop giving out so many messages, even in my own head, and not taking in so many.

7. • Holy Leisure means doing everything slowly, attentively and only when it's worth doing. Smell the flowers!
   - Self-acceptance: I am not all that terrific and I don't have to be.
   - All will be well and all manner of things shall be well (Jesus via Julian of Norwich)
   - God's love is first – being accepted (unconditionally) comes before doing OK!
   - Life is never simple.

8.   ———

9 • When your rhythm is disrupted consider your lifestyle!
   - sleeping, exercise, relaxation, recreation, diet
   - honesty, selfishness, morality
   - spiritual disciplines
   - Remember the Jesus Prayer
   - Remember Spiritual Reading

10 • Engage with the symbolic
   - Be creative using God-given awareness
   - Be intrinsic: tolerant, open to new ideas
   - 'I just look at God and let God look at me.' (Peasant of Ars)

11. • Seek a Spiritual Friend, wisely
    • Listen to God

12. • Second-hand faith never lasts the distance!
    • Prayer is a progressive activity that leads to still waters and a sharper awareness, which I can carry into everything I say and do.
    • Everyone has mystical qualities

13. • Find some sacred space, wherever you are.
    • Practise Detachment – towards God, self and others.

14. • It is not easy to hear from God, but neither is it difficult – but beware; move slowly and evaluate.
    • Commit to what God seems to say.
    • If there is no sin in your life, prayer is dry, and God is calling but seems miles away; if you feel strangely depressed but not abandoned really then: relax, ride the wave, allow God to be in charge and at God's time come out of it feeling a changed person. You've had a dark night of the soul period.

15. • Never give up on the last goal.
    • The end result may be known, but there still is an opposition on the field.
    • Always stay connected with the coach
    • Always read both a spiritual book and one for relaxation.
    • Spend time in church(es)
    • Share of substance, talent and forgiveness
    • Listen to people and really hear their stories.

Authors Worth Reading

(See also footnote references to specific works, throughout this book).

Richard Foster
Thomas H. Green
Morton Kelsey
Kenneth Leech
Brennan Manning
Thomas Merton
Calvin Miller
Thomas Moore
Henri Nouwen
Eugene Peterson
Richard Rohr
David Tacey
Jean Vanier
Philip Yancey

Epilogue

From: *emma@latestisp.com*
To: *Joe*
Subject: *God*

Hi Joe,

Having a ball. Michelangelo much to blame for God being an old man in the sky. Can't relate to that. Thanks, once again, for making me see. Italy is wonderful.

Much love,
Emma.

Appendix: Walking the Walk

You are probably familiar with the idea of not just 'talking the talk' but of actually 'walking the walk'. Emma and Joe both are 'walking the walk', although it took Emma a little time getting to that, which is understandable. The invitation is to you as well, to start walking. Or perhaps, depending on your experience in spiritual matters, to continue and walk further. In that case the following pages should be helpful.

The story of Joe and Emma is based on a series of lectures in Christian Spirituality that is held yearly at Tabor College in Adelaide, in South Australia. Much discussion takes place during these hours and the students are encouraged to practise set exercises at home. Generally it changes their lives, at least to some extent. Many comment that they had no idea about the rich tradition of the Christian Church in spirituality and the options that are available to them. 'Why didn't we know this?' is a frequent question.

Meeting Emma is suitable for personal study, for group discussion, and for retreats. It could be a continual companion on the road of spiritual experience, for there is so much to learn that you are unlikely to find the ideas presented ever to have been fully mastered. But at any level of expression the blessings will be bountiful. The key is to visit and then revisit. Spiritual experience is never static and a continual engagement will result in different outcomes even with the same exercise. It is well worth persevering with.

Every concept that Joe introduces to Emma is found in mainstream Christianity and has been tested and proven helpful over many hundreds of years. The instructions and ideas presented in the remainder of this book are to facilitate your personal growth, and enhance your relationship with God. This section includes some additional comments and suggestions on how a vibrant spiritual life might be maintained. It does not, however, replace the information contained in the narrative section of the book. It would be wise to keep paying close attention to the ideas and concepts that each chapter of *Meeting Emma* introduces.

Under the heading 'Questions for reflection and discussion' you will find for each chapter ideas that can be brought to prayerful reflection and/or be discussed in small groups. It may be helpful to keep a record of your findings. There should be a desire not simply to talk about matters, but to start practising some of the ideas.

The best way is to start slowly and at the beginning. You will have noticed that the events between Emma and Joe have a certain progression. After all, Emma at first has little idea what Joe is introducing her to. So, begin with 'Coffee' in chapter 1 – and possibly a real cup of coffee – and comfortably settle in. Don't be in a hurry. Rather, take your time and make sure you enjoy the discoveries you are bound to be making. Once a firm foundation of reflective prayer has been established, it is possible to become more selective with the exercises. You will find that some suit you more than others. Focus on those particularly and return to them often. However, make sure also to attend to exercises that seem more difficult. You will need that for personal development.

By all means feel free to contact me at (mspyker@adelaide.tabor.edu.au) with any questions or comments you may have.

1 Coffee

During their first cup of coffee together Joe raises with Emma the question of 'being before doing'. That is with good reason. Spirituality is firstly concerned with being, from which the doing will then flow forth. Doing reflects being, of course, and the two are closely connected, for as Jesus said, 'Good fruit comes from a good tree' (cf. Matt. 7:16–20). An important criterion of the quality of a person's spirituality in Christian tradition is whether it results in acts of mercy and kindness. If not, the spirituality of that person may be considered questionable.

However, in our busy lives, we don't often assign much time to getting in touch with ourselves. So our spirituality develops, or possibly stagnates, separately from our immediate consciousness. That is not a good situation. Without personal effort I will not grow spiritually. So, where is a good place to start?

First of all, learn to be solely with yourself and give that sufficient time each day. You cannot really be with yourself meaningfully if your attention is taken up by a myriad of activities and distractions. You will need to find a quiet place. You can also not be with yourself truly if thoughts are spinning around in your head willy-nilly like a carousel at a fairground. A concerted effort is needed to bring all that to a stop, at least during the times you spend seeking the privacy of reflection. That process begins with relaxation, with a determined effort of slowing down. Spirituality of the inner self in relation with God commences with 'the glory of being alone', and at rest.

If you find it difficult to be alone, because restless and possibly negative thoughts and anxieties tend to crowd your mental and emotional space, please understand that this is a very common problem. It is also a clear indication that you should persevere, for these disturbances will begin to reduce greatly in strength and frequency when you take regular time out with God. Jesus promised to set us free, and becoming free from the negativity and unrest that dwells in us surely belongs to that promise. If the results aren't immediately obvious, please don't allow yourself to become discouraged. You can be sure that God will meet you effectively, and is doing so, even if it doesn't always seem that way. That is the experience of many who have gone before.

Relaxation

For a reflective spirituality it is essential that you cultivate the skill of relaxation. It is often suggested that the best position to relax in is on your back. You can, however, relax quite well while sitting up. It may depend on how you feel and your circumstances. But whatever the case, it is important that you are comfortable and that your body has a good posture. You may wish to play some appropriate music as long as it does not affect your ability to come to rest mentally, to a point where the music can remain unnoticed.

The problem with relaxing is that the body and mind tend to object, particularly in the beginning. You might wish to stretch a little to release some tension. Relaxing properly is not all that easy. It needs concentration at first. You might focus on the various parts of your body, beginning with the feet and legs. You will probably find that they are not quite relaxed, and you should purposely relax deeper; make your legs fall through the floor, so to speak.

Work up towards your head and particularly make sure that your facial muscles are losing their rigidity. The face tends to have a set expression, frequently influenced by tensions that can have a considerable grip. This also affects the head muscles and the neck. You may wish to roll your head a few times.

Once you are relaxed bodily you could say a simple prayer quietly in your mind. For instance: 'The Lord is my Shepherd, I shall not want.' Just repeat that for a while, slowly. You may then follow that by using the words, 'Jesus leads me besides still waters.' The aim is to become more conscious of the presence of God and to steer your mental processes away from your daily concerns. Once you feel really restful, you can try to cease prayer and to stop thinking altogether, coming into a mode of 'simply being'. Perhaps you will fall asleep. That wouldn't be so bad. The best sleeps are those in the presence of the Lord.

When ending your relaxation, please do so slowly. Take your time getting up, try to move about a little less urgently for a while, and seek to keep your thoughts on God and on your concerns in life in the presence of God. It might well be that you will receive some insights. Small insights can be very valuable.

You may decide to keep a record of significant insights that are derived from your reflections and discussions, and return to these when helpful.

Questions for reflection and discussion

- What are the reasons for finding it difficult to allocate sufficient time for relaxation in my lifestyle and getting in touch with myself?
- Perhaps I'll start regular relaxation, but then I will probably stop. How may continuation be ensured?

- It is not the relaxation that is the main purpose but the connectedness with God. Why is relaxation so important in this process?

2   Who Is It, That I Am?

I am sure that every person struggles with the question of, 'Who exactly am I?' Of course, there is no clear answer. Personhood is far too complicated for simple explanations. That is reflected in the billions spent each year on helping people to sort themselves out, at least to the point where they can cope with life. For that is what most of us are doing as best we can: coping with our daily existence. It's what life is like.

Joe is beginning to explain this to Emma and has some valuable insights to share. Foundational to his understanding is the idea taught by Thomas Merton, and many others, that generally our self-realisation is conditioned by our experiences since childhood. For instance, if I learned early in life that being clever gives me brownie points, then cultivating the 'being clever' act will help my security and acceptance considerably. Life, that way, becomes more manageable. There is then of course always the fear of failing in cleverness and the anxieties that can bring.

Merton further insists, and here he has far less in common with those in the psychological helping professions, that apart from this *false* self we are invited to find our *true* self in Jesus Christ, which is of an altogether different nature. It is the person I really am, if only I could break through the barriers of social conditioning, and with the help of God put on the nature of Christ. In Christ my unique self, which dwells within me potentially but is insufficiently shaped, is waiting to come forth. Being my *true* self, I will experience wholeness and real freedom. Of course a full realisation of this will only be achieved when I am in heaven, but the invitation is for right now, this day, today, and there is much to be gained. One of the books by Merton that may be particularly helpful regarding personhood, religion and spiritual dynamics is *Seeds of Contemplation.*[1]

Becoming more truly self-aware and also more accepting of yourself is best accomplished by spending quality time with God, in which you do not set the agenda. Don't bring a host of issues before God, if any at all, except perhaps some honest questions about yourself. Occasionally it can happen that, when quiet before God, some issues will be raised that you are not aware of, but which God is concerned with. Whenever God reveals, it is done in a way that communicates love and acceptance. Accusation is the devils' business and you should always withstand that in your spirit. But likewise, always try to face up and follow through what is revealed in love by God. It helps release your *true* self.

Continue with your relaxation. When you are calm, focus in your spirit on the Lord Jesus Christ. Imagine looking towards him, but don't work too hard at doing so. Just let it happen. Express your love towards him – your failing, well-intentioned love, that is so feeble – but it is sufficient and all he would ask for. Then try perceiving the responses that come your way. It may be intuition, an idea, a realisation, an understanding or something else. If what you are discovering is significant, make sure you give it the attention it deserves once your time with God is finished.

---

[1] Thomas Merton, *Seeds of Contemplation* (Anthony Clarke, 1972)

Questions for reflection and discussion

- What might be some of the messages that have conditioned me?
- What are some of my major psycho-spiritual needs, and what desires do these press upon me? (This is quite an in-depth personal question, which you may wish to leave alone for a while. It is definitely not meant for group discussion. But it is worth mentioning, for it is an important question.)
- Why might listening to God be more difficult than talking to God?
- Joe explains to Emma that God's Spirit is always engaged with the Christian, whatever her or his actions. Why is this an important realisation?
- Respond prayerfully to the lines of poetry by St John of the Cross, that Joe wrote out for Emma.

3   The Invitation

Emma is invited to come closer to God and this presents her with a decision. Will she accept the invitation? It is not just a matter of saying 'Yes' to God, but of reaching out and giving it the needed time in her day. Because of her many activities and interests, that will be a challenge. Time will need to be set aside, and she would need to learn the language God communicates in, a language easily crowded out by the mutter and stutter of everyday life.

At this point it might be helpful to mention the discipline of simplicity. Many people through the ages, of all nationalities and beliefs, have felt that if only life could be kept simple, it would be enhanced and reveal its beauty more easily. This interest is further kept burning by the realisation that simplicity offers a person more self-determination, for it liberates from many of the unnecessary cultural demands that life brings.

Christianity has a rich tradition of simplicity. Richard Foster's book *Freedom of Simplicity*[2] makes for valuable reading and the chapter on simplicity in his book *Celebration of Discipline*[3] is also very worthwhile. A verse from a Shaker hymn reads:

'Tis a gift to be simple, 'tis a gift to be free,
    'Tis the gift to come down where we ought to be.
And when we find ourselves in the place just right,
    'Twill be in the valley of love and delight![4]

The Shakers, of course, are famous for the majestic simplicity of their architecture and furniture. It is deeply spiritual, pure, balanced – in fact, somehow just perfect. It is interesting that their hymn speaks of coming down to where we ought to be, and that being a gift of God. As with all things spiritual for the Christian, it can only be achieved in partnership with Jesus.

Simplicity with God is not just a matter of getting rid of the clutter in our lives and the many meaningless activities that come our way every week. It also means sharpening our spiritual focus and aligning our attitudes with those taught by Jesus. Coming down to where we ought to be, might well be translated as 'getting down from our high horse' into the meeker valleys of the Lord.

From a truly spiritual perspective it can be said that if our aim is Jesus exclusively, then many of life's questions and decisions, when brought under the banner of 'Seeking

---

[2] Richard Foster, *Freedom of Simplicity* (HarperCollins, 1981)

[3] Richard Foster, *Celebration of Discipline* (HarperCollins, 1983)

[4] D.E. Shi, *In Search of the Simple Life: American Voices, Past and Present* (Gibbs Smith, 1986), 73

first the Kingdom', could be resolved fairly quickly. That is a major challenge though; one to remember, but not one to become despondent with. Just keep persevering. Surely you shall win a few.

So, Emma faces her invitation, the call of becoming more intimate with God. It is an invitation to us all. Intimacy takes time and focus; it also asks for exclusivity. You can only be intimate with a few people and then only if you give them your undivided attention. It is this undivided attention that is helped by the discipline of simplicity, not just with God, but also with people and in relating to your own self.

Questions for reflection and discussion

- How can I realistically simplify my life to allow for more quality time with God?
- It is difficult to first 'Seek the Kingdom'. What might be the significant dynamics in my personal make-up that might restrict me in this, and is there anything I could do about it? Write your thoughts down for future reference.
- Unreasonable attachments to material possessions, or ideas about oneself, e.g. status, might enslave a person. Are there such areas in my life? How can I best hand these over to God and still enjoy my possessions, but be free of unhelpful attachments? Make some notes.
- How do I respond to the idea of being intimate with God – small, imperfect me and a huge, awesome God? It seems entirely possible, for many believers have experienced it. But is it really for me?
- Genuine intimacy requires openness. In what way might I be more open with Jesus?

4 Meaning, Identity and Solitude

Getting to know God better also means getting to know myself better. It helps in the development of my identity, of knowing who I am. The process is slow, but over the years it really strengthens the core of my being. It is not easy to figure out who I am and what I am here for. The questions keep coming and that is unlikely to stop altogether. But as long as the issues at stake are not deeply foundational, challenging the core of my personhood, and are rather those concerned with my daily existence and the confusion that might bring, I am safe. God is in the business of providing that safety, a place where I am known and accepted and find belonging. Jesus promised that he would prepare that place for anyone seeking it.

Emma, in her twenties, will struggle with the question of meaning and self-identification. It is the right time in her life to address these issues seriously. Joe explains about meaning and the 'Who am I?' question. He also makes it clear that the answer is best found in and with Jesus. As he says: 'Without God I cannot really become myself properly.' It is this quest for meaning, for a framework of human understanding in which the frequently perplexing questions of life can be placed, that leads people on a search after God. It is God's call to the human spirit that initiates the stepping out on a spiritual journey in which the traveller will find both joys and difficulties. Soon the challenge is: How best to remain eager and energetic?

Joe explains about the Desert Fathers and Desert Mothers who thought to solve the problem by leaving society and, as Australians would say, 'going bush' – away from it all, into solitude and the simple life of prayer and adoration. Of course, it wasn't quite that simple. Their stories tell of significant spiritual struggles resulting in great wisdom. What happened was recorded at the time – Helen Waddell's book *The Desert Fathers* offers an English version.[5] But you will find the short book *The Way of the Heart*, by Henri Nouwen,[6] an easier read and very contemporary. Henri takes ideas central to desert spirituality, such as solitude and silence, and uses a number of Desert Fathers' stories and sayings in applying them to modern life. It is very perceptive writing.

If you would be interested to read a recent account of someone visiting the places in Egypt where the Desert Fathers and Mothers lived, you should obtain a copy of James Cowan's *Journey to the Inner Mountain*.[7] James is an accomplished Australian writer who, to his surprise, found another Australian living in solitude very close to the cave of St Antony, considered the founder of the desert movement. The book includes good historical and theological perspectives and wrestles with the question of integrating the 'wisdom of the desert' into our current lifestyles.

Joe introduces Emma to the concept of solitude. 'Without solitude we will remain victims of our society,' Nouwen writes. Solitude starts with being alone with God and can result in carrying God's presence knowingly with me into my daily activities. Somehow this presence creates a kind of buffer between myself and the world. I am fully engaged in my activities, but remain slightly distanced from it all the same. At least, enough to help me with my objectivity and with being more firmly in control

[5] H. Waddell, (tr.), *The Desert Fathers* (Vintage Spiritual Classics, 1998: UK edn Fontana, n. d.)

[6] H. Nouwen, *The Way of the Heart* (London: Daybreak, 1990)

[7] James Cowan, *Journey to the Inner Mountain* (Hodder and Stoughton, 2002)

of my life and the pressures it brings. This control, and the equilibrium it gives, will assist me in my ability to practise kindness and understanding. It is existentially attractive but, as Joe admits, not easily achieved. Still, relating to God in private regularly, for good periods of time, is bound to bring results. Solitude is important.

Questions for reflection and discussion

- Where does the 'meaning' in my life, as I have found it thus far, originate? How did I find it?
- How do I deal every day with the question of 'what am I about?'
- How have I arrived at a sense of belonging, if at all? What might be the best way of talking to God about it? What are my desires here?
- Practising solitude obviously is a long-term process. How might I facilitate this discipline?
- Being in solitude with God does not necessarily need to happen in the prayer closet. What are the many other places in which I might enjoy God's presence privately?

5   The Prayer Spectrum

Prayer is mystery. It opens up a realm of activity in which there are dynamics that are very different from ordinary life. But God's Word encourages me to enter into that realm and do so frequently. When Joe, in his e-mail to Emma, explains the Prayer Spectrum, he merely tries to give a broad overview of the kind of activities that prayer allows for. On the one side you have the 'doing' prayers such as Intercession and Spiritual Warfare. On the other side is praying that engages more with 'being', like Meditation and Contemplation. What Joe describes as

Worship, for want of a better word (for each prayer expression involves worship, of course), fits in the middle of the Spectrum.

It would be worthwhile reading Joe's explanation carefully. In your prayer times you will then be more aware of the options available and may better sense the various movements in your spirit. As the person praying you can control much of the process. However, the urge and ability to pray will not originate exclusively from your spirit, but also to a large extent from God. Central to all effective prayer is a realisation that the process begins with God, with the interaction of the Holy Spirit with your own spirit.

Many Christians find difficulty in locating the Holy Spirit within their spiritual awareness. God can be recognised as the Wholly Other, who yet can be known even if only partially. Jesus once came as a human being, so that allows for reasonable identification. But what about the third Person in the Trinity, the Holy Spirit? The Bible is clear about the Holy Spirit being God and of a personal and relational nature. But, how do I deal with that? Is the Holy Spirit perhaps mostly ignored in my life?

It is an important question. When I pray, my prayers involve the Holy Spirit as someone who is active in my life. I can, of course, easily ignore that reality. God will understand this oversight and it is not a major problem. It reveals, however, an unfortunate lack of awareness, possibly due to the conceptual difficulties I might have in dealing with a God who is Three in One.

The concept of Trinity can indeed be confusing. Particularly so, if you take an analytical approach and you need to see everything neatly explained. That is bound to end in failure, as it always does when dealing with authentic mysteries. Mystery in its very nature (and this is what I like about it) is not properly explainable and thus leaves me the freedom of reaching beyond explanations. It is often much more fun to be intuitive. If I have difficulty in getting my (proverbial) head around the concept of Trinity, which the Bible presents to me as a true spiritual reality, then at least I can open my heart to it and enjoy the wonder. For example, if God is called Father – and why not Mother? – while actually being without gender and well worthy of the name Eternal Parent, let me enter that mystery and relate to God in the way I feel I can best handle these revelations

So, what about the Holy Spirit, with whom, the Apostle Paul tells me, I am in continual partnership? It is simple. I must increase my awareness of this senior partner in the relationship and give due recognition. The very Life of God in my life originates with the Spirit. It is the Spirit of Love and Help and Hope, who is personally interested in my well-being and growth. As the father said to Jesus about the healing of his child, 'I believe; Lord, help my unbelief.'

Questions for reflection and discussion

- Which ideas in the Prayer Spectrum particularly interest me? How might I better engage with these in prayer?
- How do I respond to the idea that just sitting quietly focused before God without saying anything much, and seemingly doing nothing, is actually prayer?
- What, in my view, should the outcome of a good prayer time be – and what if it doesn't happen?
- What do I actually know about the Holy Spirit?
- How might I begin to relate better to the Holy Spirit?

6   Presence, Places and Silences

A sense of belonging is a deeply emotional and spiritual
yearning in everyone's life. It can be glossed over and it
may very well be disguised in some people, but the fact
remains: to be psycho-spiritually healthy, one needs to
belong. And it is this sense of belonging that forms the
basis on which security can be built, which in turn allows
for maturation and personal growth. However, that sense
of belonging is given by others and cannot be obtained
properly in any other way. Others are the ones to give me
a place, and hopefully that will happen. It means having a
significant place with family, with friends, at work and of
course with God, who is the foremost place-maker. I
myself should also be a place-maker in my turn.

A related factor is self-acceptance. Joe explains all this
to Emma and encourages her to feel OK about herself with
good reason. Every life has baggage to carry along; and it
is the dynamics of spiritual growth in Jesus Christ that
help me deal with this effectively over a period of time.
God will work in the depth of my soul, and I can assist the
process by adhering to the disciplines that Christian spirituality has on offer. I must allow time for that, for finding
God and consequently also myself.

Personal space is not easily come by in our busy world.
Previously Joe mentioned solitude and now he introduces
the concept of silence. Again, the little book *The Way of the
Heart* by Henri Nouwen[8] is a valuable text on this. It is
simple, practical and insightful. Henri believes that it
is not always helpful to talk to everyone about everything,
which is a kind of modern phenomenon. There is considerable value in a measure of privacy and self-containment

---

[8] H. Nouwen, *The Way of the Heart* (London: Darton, Longman
and Todd, 1981)

for it harnesses the energy needed to speak significantly when appropriate.

In books on spirituality the concept of silence appears frequently. It is a kind of bedrock necessity to all who wish to progress in meditative and contemplative practices. But quite apart from that, even when living a life that does not include these, it is still essential to have enough silence in each day, if only for getting into meaningful contact with yourself. The adrenalin of life, and everything that crowds in around us, restricts our silences, and moments of quiet need to be wrested back from the visual and verbal onslaughts we experience.

Joe has much to say about it and gives some good advice. You might wish to try it out. If you find what Joe suggests to Emma difficult, then please persevere a little. Some people may be quieter by nature than others, but all will need moments of internal privacy. These moments will enhance the ability of listening; not just to God, but also to yourself; and also, quite significantly so, the ability of listening to other people.

Questions for reflection and discussion

- How do I feel about belonging? Everyone is 'adrift' to some extent, but do I have places where I am welcome to drop my anchor?
- How am I doing with self-acceptance, knowing that I am not perfect, but OK? Have I ever discussed this with God?
- Could I list some of the 'baggage' that I might be carrying in my life? What might be a way of dealing with this more effectively?
- Which of the ideas about silence that Joe discusses with Emma are particularly of interest to me? Why might that be and how could I respond meaningfully?

- Why might listening better to God and to myself enhance my ability to listen to others?

7 Holy Leisure

When Joe considers that he has to fight for his sanity, he is feeling mentally and emotionally over-stimulated and stretched. In fact his soul has lost control of his day, even if he may manage the tasks at hand successfully. There will be a hurriedness and lack of clear focus in all he does, including the times with God, and an avoidable draining away of much energy. It is the story of a modern urgent lifestyle, attractive perhaps because of the power dynamics that may be in play or the ego-satisfaction on offer, but unhelpful when aiming for a balanced spirituality. The problem is not new. That's why the Church Fathers spoke of *otium sanctum* or 'holy leisure'.

Calvin Miller in his book *The Table of Inwardness*[9] mentions this discipline and refers to it as 'true leisure in the middle of a busy life'. It can be an antidote to the emptiness in our lives, the partial disintegration of our personhood. Joe's reflections on the idea describe it adequately, and you might wish to consider designing your own 'holy leisure' day regularly. Of course, ideally every day should be approached with 'holy leisure'. There are no reasons why that couldn't be possible, apart from the demanding, persuasive rhythms of modern life. Somehow we have convinced ourselves that being busy is necessary, normal and unavoidable, even if in the process much of our energy is directed ineffectively. There is much to be learned here.

---

[9] Calvin Miller, *The Table of Inwardness* (Marshall Pickering, 1987)

From his reflections you will notice that Joe tries to take a 'down-to-earth' approach with his faith and is no fool about how easily the ideal can be diminished by the convenient. Keeping up a minimum standard is a struggle. He reminds himself to keep making a positive difference in places, to do some good. If he isn't overly successful God will not accuse him but will rather encourage towards a better effort. Helping others (and the options are always many) is a serious business in which 'holy leisure' becomes rather essential as it urges, when necessary, for the important to have priority over the urgent. That is quite an achievement in this modern life, where increasing numbers of superficial matters clamour for immediate attention.

One particular thought of Joe's deserves a few comments. It concerns the psycho-spiritual dynamic of committing your life to a cause greater than yourself in order to find significant meaning. It is a basic human need that has generated many ideologies and causes throughout history. The nature of the cause determines to a large extent the mood of the adherent. Angry causes make for angry people. Humanitarian causes develop caring people. People without a cause tend to end up with themselves as the primary reason for living with all the related psychological tragic consequences. As Christians we are fortunate in having a perfect cause in Jesus Christ and his gospel. It is best not to be lukewarm about it. The healthy way forward is to take the gospel seriously.

Questions for reflection and discussion

• What might prevent me from having a 'holy leisure' day?

- Do I have a 'sanity' speedometer? At what point am I over the speed limit and need slowing down? If I don't, what might the speeding ticket read like?
- What are the common circumstances and attitudes that could prevent me from doing some good?
- How frequently does the urgent overshadow the important in my life? In which areas mostly? What could be done about it as an overall approach rather than a piecemeal one?
- Why do I think it is true that a person needs a cause larger than him- or herself? How am I personally doing with this?

8   The Dream

Calvin Miller in *The Table of Inwardness* relates a moving story of how a priest witnesses a tragic accident in which a number of persons are incinerated in a car. He kneels on the pavement and prays. Miller explains that the priest at that moment is *Christifying* the tragedy. To many that may have seemed of little use, but from a Christian perspective it was surely the correct response. It was a vicarious act in which a servant of the Lord saw with the eyes of Christ and interceded while being overcome by the moment. In human life the moments of vulnerability are plentiful with some having deadly consequences. God then is present. It is not for me to understand everything about that reality but to accept it, with faith, as being true. With our backs against the wall there is a God at that wall as well. It's a given for the Christian and the foundation of belief.

When Emma faces the death of a friend, she wonders how such a senseless accident can ever lead to worthwhile prayer, but then concludes that if senseless and abhorrent events are a legitimate hurdle to prayer, who would ever pray? For the world abounds in tragedies. Her prayer didn't work very well during those days of the funeral, or at least didn't seem to. But she was trying, and the dream showed that God had not forgotten her. Maturity comes to life from such moments of difficulty.

In Emma's dream a wolf is following her. Every person has a wolf or two in the closet. It represents the dynamics that encourage me to remain my own person rather than hand matters over to the Lord. It is the ego side of life, the fearsome side, the one laden with anxieties, menace and pride. It is the side we have nevertheless befriended in our small-mindedness and need for self-determination. The defiant cry of 'I'm an individual' may seem powerful, but actually reflects considerable psychological immaturity. The song that proudly croons, 'I did it my way', may be fine when in your twenties, but it becomes a rather pathetic statement at an older age when emotional needs such as 'doing my own thing' should have been overcome. All this, and more, is potentially following Emma in light of her future. She senses that, but cannot put it into words. However, her response in the situation is more important than her understanding of it.

In Emma's dream, overcoming the wolf means walking out of the valley. Such valleys are part of everyone's life and there is only one good way of escaping: start climbing out of it with Jesus. First of all allow him to help you recognise the valley. In that short-sightedness common to all, it might remain undetected. Whatever you discover, don't fight it. If it is revealed in the love of God, and not through thoughts full of accusation that might reflect a dislike of yourself in certain areas, discuss it with the Lord and work on positive change. The Holy Spirit will help you. Again, as with all spiritual growth, it is the road to freedom.

Questions for reflection and discussion

- What might be the best spiritual approach towards the suffering in the world and the goodness of an almighty God?
- If I disagree with God, should I discuss this in prayer or just leave it, and why?
- Is there a wolf in my life that can easily be identified? If not, might there be one I cannot see? Or, perhaps there isn't one. How might this problem be best addressed?
- If there is a wolf, how do I determine whether God is revealing this or whether I am reflecting negativity about myself into the problem? Or, could it be that I am ignoring the wolf with the excuse that it is just negative thinking? How can I test this?
- How do I best climb out of a valley? How long might it take?

9   Centring Prayer and Spiritual Reading

Bodily health helps spiritual health. In my life, I find it necessary to stay reasonably fit, eat properly and get enough sleep. I also need my leisure time. I have a busy job, with always a few private projects on the go – like writing this book – and I love being a husband, father and grandfather. And there is more, and 'it's all beautiful', as a friend of mine would say. And so it is. But there must be a balance to avoid crashing to a grinding halt. That starts with fitness and moderation.

Emma experiences the negative effects of a life that has lost its rhythm. 'Have a few good sleeps', Joe advises her, 'and look after your body.' It simply is the best spiritual advice. When you are unfit, it is a struggle to become fitter particularly so in the beginning. When your sleep is restless, it needs working on. Diet, exercise and relaxation all play a part. So does reflective spirituality. Ever since the apostle Paul described human beings as having a body, soul and spirit it seems as if each person consists of three parts. That is not true. I am *one* person and my body, soul and spirit are *one*, inseparable and undivided. Even in a mystical trance, my spirit is still one with my body, for if not, I would have died and ceased being human.

Consider the unity of body, soul and spirit a reflection of the Trinity, if you like. The point is that for it to function well, each needs to be kept reasonably healthy. It means that going for a swim is as good for my spirit and soul as prayer might be. When I am unfit, a swim or walk is probably the very best that could happen. When irritated, it is quite spiritual to put on a CD and enjoy some music that changes my soul dynamics and gives release. I'm sure you understand where I am coming from. It is not difficult to get the picture. It is harder to live it out. But we should, really, be looking after the whole person.

One way in which life can remain more focused and less disintegrated is centring prayer. Joe explains the idea and mentions the Jesus Prayer in particular: 'Lord Jesus Christ, Son of God, have mercy on me a sinner.' You may wish to read Joe's instructions to Emma and try it for yourself. You may create your own prayer, or be given one by the Lord that is particularly helpful for a season. The key is to engage with the idea of praying without ceasing. Of course you will often cease, but it is good to keep applying the prayer method whenever it comes to mind. Try not to give up on it too quickly. However, if it doesn't work, please don't worry. Some find great benefit in it, others don't. It's personal and what works for one may not for another.

You may also wish to try the *lectio divina*. Again, Joe explains it quite well. Take note of the dynamics of discovery, evaluation and application involved in the process. It is important to have times in which Scripture is approached using a method of praying and reading that brings insight and revelation. Martin Luther, in praying through the Commandments, used to reflect first on what God required of him and would then find reasons for thanksgiving. Next, he made his confession and finally expressed a prayer of petition. Walter Trobisch, in a small booklet called *Martin Luther's Quiet Time*,[10] suggests that this approach can be used for reflective reading of the Bible as well. Select a text and ask, 'What am I grateful for?' (Thanksgiving). Next, 'What do I regret?' (Confession). Then, 'What should I ask for?' (Prayer concerns). And finally, 'What shall I do?' (Action). Luther encourages pen and paper to be at hand.

Questions for reflection and discussion

- In what ways can I bring more balance into my life, caring for body, soul and spirit?
- Why is it such a challenge to achieve balance, and what might be an answer to dealing with it adequately on a consistent basis?
- Centring prayer helps towards maintaining equilibrium in spirit and soul. How might that be?
- What is so powerful about the theology expressed in the Jesus Prayer? How do these words affect me?
- What is attractive about a reflective, prayerful reading of Scripture? Why should it definitely be part of the spiritual disciplines I practise?

---

[10] Walter Trobisch, *Martin Luther's Quiet Time* (Editions Trobisch, 1977)

10 Symbols, Art and Creativity

In his introduction to *Life of Pi*, Yann Martel writes,

> If we citizens do not support our artists, then we sacrifice our imagination on the altar of crude reality and we end up believing in nothing and having worthless dreams.[11]

It is a wonderful comment. Though written about Western culture in general, it is a warning for the Christian life. It is highly unlikely that the church will end up believing in nothing, but there are plenty of past churchgoers who would place themselves under that description, even if it might not be fully correct. It is a tragic situation.

What might 'the altar of crude reality' be like in the church? Could it represent the rational, the functional and the expedient? Or maybe the organisational and political, when it holds an upper hand on the spiritual, creative, symbolic and mystical? It will depend on the situation you are facing. Whatever the case, if the church is to avoid a religion of mostly rules, methods and works, it must make sure to foster the intuitive and artistic. That's where worthwhile dreams, rather than the worthless ones mentioned by Martell, originate. Fortunately the rising interest in spirituality throughout society urges the church in the right direction.

However, concluding that the spiritual cannot be rational or practical would be wrong. Rationality is a necessary safeguard and very beneficial when used wisely. It supports the spiritual with its ability to explain the things of God. Frameworks are necessary in the spiritual life, which cannot flourish if void of structure. Foundations of understanding and logic are needed to build

[11]   Yann Martel, *Life of Pi* (Canongate, 2001), xii

on. But by definition a foundation is underneath and not prominent. The beauty of a building is found in its design, its colour and its artistry. God is both a builder and an artist. Just look around in creation if you need convincing. God's people, likewise, should be both; they build and aim for artistic expression in all they do.

Joe's lecture covers a broad range of topics related to this – from symbols, to icons and art in general. It is important for Christians to be exposed to activities of worship that include windows to the sensual and intuitive. The rational as well as the nurturing side of personality must be catered for, the masculine *and* the feminine. The side that gives a person the most struggles will need some extra attention if a balanced spirituality is to be gained. As Joe explains, the artistic is necessary for modes of expression and experience that are not otherwise possible. The non-rational is essential to spiritual growth.

Questions for reflection and discussion

- How might I best engage with the artistic around me? Have I ever sat with a painting, poem or musical piece and allowed it to get under my skin? I might decide to use a picture of spiritual significance occasionally. What is my experience of the symbolic?
- Perhaps the rational and organisational doesn't come easy. Why would it be worthwhile developing those abilities a little more? How might God be of help?
- How would I describe my ability to be creative, just for fun – not for profit – and what place does it have in my lifestyle?
- Interaction with nature, with God in attendance, helps the intuitive side of a person. What are my experiences here?

- Joe encourages his students to become better aware, to see more clearly as Jesus would. How does he feel improvement can come about and what is my response to this?

11   Spiritual Friends

Spiritual Friendship has a long tradition. If a good spiritual friend can be found, such a relationship will be very beneficial. Unfortunately the question is often where to meet that person, for they don't seem to be around much. That could be true, as meeting for a spiritual friendship 'session' requires at least some understanding of the process. Fortunately instructions about that are more easily come by these days. Training usually is available somewhere if you search for it, and a good number of books can be purchased. Recently I came across a new one by David Benner entitled *Sacred Companions*.[12] David writes on spirituality from a counselling perspective but, as always, is informative and very readable.

Two of the books that have been available for years are *Soul Friend* by Kenneth Leech[13] and *Exploring Spiritual Direction: An Essay on Christian Friendship* by Alan Jones.[14] If you like reading about the Celtic spiritual tradition you might enjoy *Soul Friendship: Celtic Insights into Spiritual Mentoring* by Ray Simpson.[15] Morton Kelsey has written

---

[12] David Benner, *Sacred Companions: The Gift of Spiritual Friendship and Direction* (Inter-Varsity Press, 2002)

[13] Kenneth Leech, *Soul Friend* (Sheldon, 1977)

[14] Alan W. Jones, *Exploring Spiritual Direction* (HarperCollins, 1983)

[15] R. Simpson, *Soul Friendship: Celtic Insights into Spiritual Mentoring* (Hodder and Stoughton, 1999)

Companions on the Inner Way[16] and there are many other books in the market place. The one I personally often refer to is *Spiritual Direction* by R. E. Morneau.[17] Unfortunately it is out of print, but perhaps you can find a copy somewhere. There are other titles and much to read, if you are interested.

Spiritual Friendship is a meeting of two people who together seek to find the mind of God mostly for one of them and not because there would be a problem to address, for Spiritual Friendship is not essentially a problem solving process like counselling or psychotherapy. But of course it may well be that in listening to God insights are received that help resolve certain matters, which is a bonus. Spiritual Friendship is suitable for all circumstances and Richard Baxter urged particularly those strong in the faith to make use of it as a way to being positively challenged in the spiritual life.

If however you are facing really difficult situations, such as frequent depression, the loss of someone close to you or of a job, it is wise to have a Spiritual Friend who besides being a spiritual person also has some psychological skills and would know when to call on professional help. Normally though, any person of spiritual maturity could make a good Spiritual Friend, particularly once having read up on the topic. Central to the process is humility and an ability to discern the movements of God in the human spirit. This matter of discernment Joe raises with Emma in chapter 14.

During a spiritual direction session it can happen that the 'director' may receive a personal word from God through insights by the 'directee'. It need not all be one-

[16] M.T. Kelsey, *Companions on the Inner Way: The Art of Spiritual Guidance* (NY: Crossroad, 1996)
[17] R.F. Morneau, *Spiritual Direction* (NY: Crossroad, 1992)

way traffic. Two people are assisting each other. Still, the focus is on the 'directee' and it is quite proper for the 'director' to challenge the other carefully regarding matters being discussed and discoveries or resolutions made in previous sessions.

Everyone should have such a Friend. If you do, please remember that it may yet be only for a season. Spiritual Friendship is not necessarily a permanent arrangement, though it should last for a while, long enough for the friends to become comfortably acquainted. Also, not everyone is suitable to be your Spiritual Friend regardless of skill and training. Personalities need to click and the relationship should flow with trust being established easily. It is a totally private interaction before God. In some cases Friends are known to switch roles with both being a 'director' at a given time. Ideally that should be in separate sessions.

Questions for reflection and discussion

- How do I rate the importance of Spiritual Friendship in the spiritual life, and why?
- If I wanted to find a Spiritual Friend, how might I best go about it?
- What might the church do to improve the availability of suitable Spiritual Friends?
- If someone were to ask me to become a Spiritual Friend, what questions might I ask of that person and also of myself?
- If I could meet a Spiritual Friend right now, which personal question would I presently bring into the listening process before God?

12   The Prayer of Awareness

When discussing the prayer of awareness Joe mentions to Emma that reaching a level at which prayer becomes more 'natural' needs determination. It simply is a matter of progression and Joe uses the teachings of St Teresa of Avila (1515–82) to explain this. A helpful book is *When the Well Runs Dry* by Thomas H. Green,[18] who has published many other titles worth reading. The idea of how to arrive at the prayer of quiet is quite fully described by Joe. In doing so he raises the idea of apophatic prayer – prayer without words or images. That kind of prayer often creates a stumbling block and the question frequently asked is, 'How can I stop thinking?' Not easily, to be honest, but it can be achieved with perseverance and God's help. It is an option that many Christians might place in the 'too hard' basket. But those who don't and have tasted of the special attraction found in quietly being with God, unencumbered by the dictates of their own thoughts, soon begin to long for it as a more permanent mode of prayer in their lives. It is the kind of prayer that, even though seemingly doing nothing much, breaks through the barriers of earthly existence.

The 'doing nothing – thinking nothing' part is deceptive, for in fact it is hard work to reach this level of inactivity and only once entered sufficiently will it stay a while, like a trance, although that word for some reason has unhelpful negative connotations. Before the deeper contemplative stage is reached, it means working hard in your spirit by concentrating your whole person on a 'simply being' activity towards God. I mean by this that you counteract your mental processes by refusing to think, which is achieved by 'looking' towards God in your

---

[18]   Thomas H. Green, *When the Well Runs Dry: Prayer Beyond the Beginnings* (Ave Maria Press, 1980), 36–55

spirit. Focused gazing is what you put your energies into, trying to see what cannot be seen, into that 'cloud' which you are quietly trying to pierce. Then at some point you can lose an awareness of self and you simply are in God's presence. God helps in this process, and without his help it cannot be achieved. Some would say that God calls a person into these prayer dynamics. Well, if it appeals to you, you may consider yourself called and God will be present helping.

Please understand that you may not necessarily receive any great revelations from this apophatic state, though at times you will. Being with God is quite a subtle experience often without form or substance. But what you will discover is that your outlook on yourself and on life will change. Joe is explaining this to Emma and considers it important. It is true, however, that this kind of prayer may not always 'work' all that well. Much depends on my state of being before I enter into it. How agitated am I, or how tired? I need to be reasonably focused and relaxed. Often the prayer of quiet only happens briefly during a prayer time. When I am being persecuted by my thoughts going all over the place and with my feelings playing havoc, it may not work at all. That's OK, for there is always next time.

One helpful hint about thoughts is that you don't have to act on them. If, for instance, the silly thought of having to buy butter at the supermarket presents itself while you are trying hard not to think at all, then don't wonder where on earth it came from, but simply drop the thought, refusing to engage with it. Also, purposefully direct your focus towards the Lord and away from thinking. Centring prayer may be helpful here. However, make sure you move on from there. All this can be learned, for part of it is a skill. The major part is God. If the prayer of awareness appeals to you I would strongly encourage you to seek after it.

Questions for reflection and discussion

- What, from Joe's explanation, do I perceive the prayer of awareness to be, and what might it achieve?
- Prayer is called the language of love. That's quite a statement. How should I approach that idea?
- In what ways might I facilitate the prayer of quiet in my life?
- Apophatic is a strange word. What is my honest reaction to it and why?
- If I were asked how I would like my prayer life to change me, what would I say?

13   Sacred Spaces and Detachment

People need sacred spaces. It may be a church, a temple, a cave, a football stadium or a lagoon. There is something about these spaces that nurtures the soul. Of course as Christians we realise that God is everywhere and is not bound to location, but nevertheless in some places God appears especially present. Whether that is really so or not is immaterial. The truth is that human spirituality seeks sacred spaces and life is poorer without these.

Emma intuitively is drawn to the cathedral. It allows her to create a distance between the world outside and herself. In this space she experiences some meaningful reflections. One is about herself as a person and the realisation that she needs more freedom from the dictates her personality is placing upon her. That is a major insight. It seems that Emma has some idea of the internal psychological dynamics that work in her life. She concludes that forgiveness is needed; and decides that she herself is a forgiving person so she'd better start forgiving. A refusal to forgive always places the person who should forgive in bondage, for it creates all sorts of negatives in the soul. It can also have that effect on those who feel not forgiven. This understanding is a cornerstone in the Christian faith for good reasons.

Another idea that appeals to Emma is the practice of Detachment. It is a key to a healthy spiritual life. Considerable bondage and restriction of soul come from the opposite of detachment, which is attachment. The latter enters our lives without much trouble at all. It is very easy to become attached to things, and ideas. I can love my car, my house, my status, my reputation, my achievements, my wealth, my religion and even my ideas about God. The list is endless. It feeds the ego. And, though it is not wrong to appreciate and enjoy things, it limits me when these become idols, objects or ideas to which I bow down and which I serve. If this seems an overstatement, please do have a think about it and see where the power is situated in these situations. Unless you can freely step away from it, the power is not completely with you.

Emma has a feel for this and was struck by the ideas of Meister Eckhart (1260–1327). His *Selected Writings* are available as a Penguin Classic,[19] but are not that easy to read. He is known for advising that even the ideas we have of God need to be treated with care. It might be helpful to try leaving these behind occasionally, for God is much larger than our limited explanations. We tend to conceptualise God according to our own preferences. There is truth in that and it is worthwhile keeping it in mind. But detachment from the many other matters in our lives is predominantly important.

---

[19] O. Davies, (tr.), *Meister Eckhart: Selected Writings* (Penguin, 1994)

For the Christian, detachment means 'handing over to God'. I bring all that has a hold on me before God and ask for release. It means that I aim at not really owning anything, but that it all belongs to God, even my very life. That is difficult because my psychology so much demands ownership in order to shape identity, which is a trap. True identity is found in Jesus Christ and so is true freedom. In 'owning nothing' I have just described the ultimate; of course I don't feel at all capable of that. But I can aim in the right direction, and I should practise a measure of detachment every day. It is a difficult task and not one that is ever fully achieved. But the principle is sound, as Emma realised. It was one of the reasons for her visiting the cathedral. She felt that help was needed and asked God for it. It takes courage to live with detachment.

Questions for reflection and discussion

- It is best not to talk about forgiveness easily. Why not?
- Is forgiveness a feeling, an attitude, a resolve, or whatever? How might I know that I have forgiven, or should I just accept that I have, if I am doing my best with it?
- Where might I find my sacred spaces? How would I make use of these?
- Which areas in my life would benefit from detachment?
- Detachment, as a lifestyle attitude, how is it best sustained – prayer of course, but what might be other ways?

14 Discernment and Dark Nights

Getting the mind of God on things is both a careful and a carefree business. Somehow, by faith and with honesty and humility, I may expect that God would speak into my life through perceptions, thoughts and feelings whenever necessary to keep me on the right track and to give the insights needed for a life of wisdom and proper focus. If I spend regular time with God, I am encouraged to live the spontaneous spiritual life and not to worry whether I might miss some obscure divine instructions that would be essential to my well-being as a Christian. God does not work in that way. Necessary 'messages' will come when needed with clarity into my mind and conscience, even if I don't recognise these as being from the Holy Spirit. It is better to be carefree in this, because anything else simply restricts the communication process anyway. Too much worry, too much care, tend to take over.

But there will be matters in life that are important enough to have lasting consequences. In that case a slow progression towards seeking insights from God in prayer and reflection is essential. These matters may concern my attitudes and mindsets, or my future and spiritual calling. It is then time for some serious investigation, if the Holy Spirit prompts towards that. I then need a gift of discernment.

A helpful book, based on the wisdom of Ignatius Loyola (1491–1556), is *Weeds among the Wheat*, by Thomas H. Green.[20] It is particularly valuable in that it doesn't give slick answers. Discernment is not a simple matter, for so much in life works against it, but nevertheless it can be achieved sufficiently and sometimes even quickly. You might wish to take a retreat one day with the aim of hearing from God. There may not be anything specific on your mind but you just would like to hear whatever God considers useful. It helps in keeping the spirit in tune with the Holy Spirit. Joe gives Emma some good advice, which you would do well to take note of.

---

[20] Thomas H. Green, *Weeds Among the Wheat – Discernment: Where Prayer and Action Meet* (Ave Maria Press, 1984)

Emma wonders about the 'dark night of the soul'. It is a significant question, for as Joe explains, the experience can come her way, if she takes God seriously. The term 'dark night' is derived from the writings of John of the Cross (1542–91). He describes an experience that has been part of spiritual growth for thousands of years. His little book of the same title, which is a section of a larger work, is readily available, but it makes for difficult and possibly confusing reading. John speaks of a 'night of the senses' and a 'night of the spirit'. It can be said that the first is what the 'dark night' would mean to us lesser mortals of spiritual desire and the second to those quite advanced in the mystical way. The 'night of the spirit', according to John, can be rather terrifying. But he isn't too clear and actually never completes the book as he intended.

In 'the night of the senses' God begins a stripping and healing process. Joe explains it adequately. Undoubtedly the concept of 'dark night' strikes a chord with people and that is understandable. The darker side of our psychology is with us all. But one should be careful not to consider major depressions automatically a 'dark night' in the sense John writes about it. Sometimes the concept is bandied about with insufficient care. It is best to check on the experience with the pointers given by Joe. Depressions, which are not 'dark nights', need dealing with differently and may require medication. But when the 'dark night' comes your way, just do what Joe suggested to Emma: 'Endure, relax and actually, if you can, enjoy a little.'

Questions for reflection and discussion

• When have I felt in need of discernment and what happened? Can I detect ways in which I might address it differently in future?

- Have I ever been on a proper retreat? Much of what is called retreat these days ends up being another 'talking session' at some place else than normal. What might be the benefits of retreating and how might I organise to join one?
- As explained, hearing from God can be carefree. How might I determine when it is time for a more concerted approach to discernment?
- What have I learned about the 'dark night' experience that is worth keeping in mind?
- What would determine whether I advise someone to work out of a negative depressing experience or ride it through with God till it stops?

15   Scoring Goals

Sharing with others from the heart, and of your possessions without reservation, is an act of love. Likewise, really listening to someone may be seen as such an act. Both sharing and listening can be difficult but, are very important, and at the centre of all meaningful relational activity. It is not difficult to accept the truth of this observation. Life bears it out.

Joe closes his conversations with Emma on these two points, sharing and listening. How well she will cope with it will largely depend on her ability to create enough spiritual space for herself in order to remain sensitive to herself and others. It further depends on her willingness to accept and work through the kind but firm dealings of God that lead to humility. That applies to all of us. Unless I become truly familiar with my own limitations, as these are covered by grace, it is difficult to accept the limitations of others generously.

Much has been written about sharing, and it is true that without a measure of authentic openness significant relationships cannot be formed. Still, that doesn't mean that it is necessary to unload your heart's feelings and thoughts indiscriminately to anyone who cares to be around. That is unwise. Henri Nouwen deplored the fact that in our modern world privacy of thought and reflection is not sufficiently appreciated. The tendency to share openly and deeply to people unknown to us needs to be approached with much caution; it can become quite counter-productive to psycho-spiritual health. My heart is not everyone's recreational playground, but a secret garden. Jean Vanier, in writing about community life, stresses the importance of finding private space and having private thoughts.[21]

Of course it is necessary to share of who you are and what you have when in the right places and circumstances. Love, without such openness and action, is not love at all. Often self-centeredness tends to get in the way. If only I could live with a complete absence of self-concern! To maintain that kind of spiritual awareness I'd do well to read up regularly on those who are less privileged. It brings my lifestyle into much-needed perspective.

Good listening is achieved by the same principles. Humility, which helps me see with godly discernment, opens the ears of my heart. Much has been written about how to listen properly and it is helpful to be well informed. But the fundamental key in the whole process is love – having a non-judgemental attitude. Being able to approach someone in that way is quite a challenge. Usually I am too full of my own ideas and preferences to

---

[21] J. Vanier, *Community and Growth* (Darton, Longman and Todd, 1989)

perceive the other person adequately. I am also full of answers, none of which is helpful in the listening process. Truly listening is difficult and few have cultivated the skill sufficiently. Joe is right in presenting it as one of the major opportunities towards a meaningful life. People, of many colours and cultures, all have their existence through Jesus Christ the Creator, whatever their beliefs and abilities. Each one deserves to be treated with dignity. Being allowed to enter a little into the life and world of another through sharing and listening is one of the wonders and privileges of being human. But it can so easily escape us, like much else that is worthwhile in life.

If the invitation extended to Emma is the same invitation you may be feeling in your heart, please be encouraged. You are asked to take the field. Whatever the challenges ahead, never give up on the next goal. As you stick to the game, whatever the weather, you will come out a winner – for sure!

The Coach will be pleased.

Questions for reflection and discussion

- Joe suggests that Emma should begin to keep a reflective journal. The same suggestion was made in Chapter 1 of this section 'Walking the Walk'. If you actually have recorded your thoughts and experiences while working through the suggested questions for reflection and discussion, what is it that strikes you most in what you have noted down?
- How would I rate myself as a listener, and in what ways might growing spiritually help me in becoming better at it?
- How do I feel when I am not being listened to adequately, and what would be the best way of dealing with this both spiritually and psychologically?

- How frequently should I read up about the poor and disenfranchised and what kind of personal responses might I consider?
- Looking back at my interaction with *Meeting Emma*, and considering the future, how might I best describe my thoughts and feelings about it?